Siblings

How to handle sibling rivalry and create lifelong, loving bonds

Linda Blair

white
LADDER

Important note

The information in this book is not intended as a substitute for medical advice. Neither the author nor White Ladder can accept any responsibility for any injury, damages or losses suffered as a result of following the information herein.

This first edition published in Great Britain in 2017 by White Ladder, an imprint of Crimson Publishing Ltd, 19–21c Charles Strcct Bath BA1 1I IX.

© Linda Blair 2017

The right of Linda Blair to be identified as the author of this work has been asserted by her in accordance with the Copyright, Designs and Patents Act, 1988.

British Library Cataloguing in Publication Data
A catalogue record for this book is available from the British Library.

ISBN 978 1 91033 625 0

Typeset by IDSUK (DataConnection) Ltd
Printed and bound in Padstow, UK By TJ International Ltd

To Paul, Becca, Judy, Penny and Christin. My rivals and my best friends all.

Contents

Contents

About the author

Linda Blair is a chartered clinical psychologist, an Associate Fellow of the British Psychological Society and a Chartered Scientist. She's worked as a clinical psychologist since 1980, both in the NHS and in private practice. She's also carried out research for the Medical Research Council and the NHS, and has published a number of academic papers. She trained at Harvard University and the Maudsley Hospital (University of London).

Linda now writes a weekly column, 'Mind Healing', for the *Telegraph*, and has written regular columns for the *Guardian*, the *Times*, the *Daily Mail* and *Psychologies* magazine. She's also published four books – this is her fifth – on child development, parenting, stress management and mindfulness. She's in great demand as a speaker, both at the corporate level and in schools and universities.

Linda lives in Bath with her husband, daughter and lively dogs.

Acknowledgements

Writing the acknowledgements makes me feel so fortunate when I think of all the people who've helped and encouraged me with my writing.

Thanks first to the many families who have come to see me in my clinics over the years, who have trusted me to help them as they struggled with various interpersonal issues. I've learned so much! Thank you all.

I learned an incredible amount about sibling relationships from my own siblings – Paul, Becca, Judy, Penny and Christin. Thanks to you all. I learned even *more* from my three wonderful children – Jonathan, Sammie and Katy. More thank yous!

How does anyone manage such a lonely profession as writing without the love and support of good friends? Thank you Frances Hedgeland, Fiona Goodwille, Paola Ehrlich, Morag Shuaib and Christin Rzasa – friend *and* sister – for always being available, always ready to listen and always ready to offer support and encouragement.

When I mention support, I think, too, of my wonderful partner Rob. I never knew a person could be so generous with their time and effort – and at the same time, so willing to be ignored for days on end while I write! Thanks, Love, for your understanding and help.

I'm a person who thinks clearly only after I've taken time to move and stretch, so I also want to say thanks to my yoga teacher Simona Hernandez, to my inexhaustible dogs Molly, Honey and Daisy, and to the staff at the Sports Training Village at the University of Bath.

I felt more confident writing this book than I've felt in the past, and that is something I owe to the authors who taught me so much during my recent creative writing course. Thank you Maggie Gee, Fay Weldon and Richard Kerridge. What inspirations you are!

This time, there's one person I wish to single out and thank especially. She is Vicki Harper, my editor at the *Telegraph*. I've worked for lots of people during my long career, but never for anyone who so wholeheartedly assumes I can 'do it'. Vicki, your confidence in me has increased my own confidence immeasurably. Thank you so much!

Acknowledgements

Finally, to make a book really work, the author needs a supportive yet critical team who are willing to work hard with her. I've certainly had that at Crimson. I offer a huge dose of gratitude to Andy Riddle, to Lyndsey Mayhew and, above all, to my editor, Beth Bishop.

What a lucky person I am!

Introduction

Imagine.

You've decided to go into town for the first time since your new baby, your second child, was born. You're walking down the main shopping street in your neighbourhood, tightly holding your enthusiastic toddler's little hand and happily telling him all about where you plan to go today. Your new baby is sound asleep, safely tucked into your baby sling.

Turning your attention away from your son, you notice some old friends approaching from the opposite direction. Immediately, you stop talking to your toddler and prepare proudly to introduce the latest member of your family. While everyone fusses over the new arrival, your overlooked toddler's sunny mood begins to fade, and he starts trying to pull you ahead impatiently. 'Come on, Mummy! Let's go!'

You pay little attention to him, delighted by your friends' admiration and approval of your baby. As your toddler's protests grow ever louder, one of your friends shakes his head knowingly and glances conspiratorially in the direction of the angry little child.

'Bet he's feeling a bit jealous,' he says, observing his increasingly frantic bids for attention.

His partner chimes in. 'Yes, the reality must be quite a shock for him ... and for you. Looks like you have your work cut out for you now! On top of taking care of two, you'll have all that sibling rivalry to deal with. Poor you!'

They wave goodbye cheerily, and you turn back to your tearful, unhappy little son. Your sunny mood has vanished. 'What have I got myself into?' you start to wonder.

Why do so many of us regard sibling rivalry in this way – particularly when, as in this example, it's so often inflamed by careless adult attitudes and behaviours? Why is the competition between brothers and sisters so often considered to be a dreadful – even shameful – problem, something to be avoided or eliminated, or if that's not possible, then minimised or dealt with as perfunctorily as possible?

Parenting books often reinforce this negative outlook. One author describes sibling rivalry as something that can't be avoided, but at least 'you can keep it to a minimum' (Ford, p. 51). Another suggests that although sibling rivalry can help kids become tougher and more resilient, at the same time it can demoralise, or even cause children 'permanent damage' (Faber and Mazlish, p. xv). The titles of books on sibling rivalry almost always suggest a negative outlook, using phrases such as 'how to stop the fighting' and 'getting beyond sibling rivalry'.

This is not the way I see sibling rivalry – or rather sibling relationships, the term I prefer to use. I consider this phenomenon to be the best set-up we have for teaching our children to become emotionally sensitive – in other words, to develop their 'EQ'.

The importance of emotional intelligence

Emotional intelligence, or EQ, a concept promoted by the psychologist and author Daniel Goleman, is the ability to recognise and understand emotional responses, both our own and those of other people, and to learn how to manage those emotions so that we can achieve our goals – and, when we choose, to help others to do the same. It's one of the most powerful assets we can have, and living with siblings means that your children will grow up in the best training ground they could have for developing this skill. Because they grow up having to share your time and attention as well as the family possessions, they'll have to learn how to negotiate and compromise when there are the inevitable conflicts of interest. Numerous studies have shown that a well-developed EQ is essential for success at work, particularly for those in leadership positions. It's also a vital ingredient for establishing and maintaining your relationships, and it's associated with good mental health and a positive outlook on life.

When children grow up with siblings, they'll also have the opportunity to experience the joy of giving and helping, and at the same time to learn to receive what others offer them, gratefully and with good grace.

Because sibling rivalry is such a powerful tool, your best approach is to make use of the occasions when it arises, rather than to try to suppress it. However, even if you did try to avoid or stamp out all instances of sibling rivalry, you'd only exhaust yourself. Your children will compete with one another no matter what you do. Sibling rivalry is not some sort of evolutionary mistake! It's unavoidable and universal. By coming to understand more about it, you'll no doubt stop dreading those occasions when your children confront one another, and start instead to welcome the opportunities to help them develop more fully.

Our relationships with our siblings are almost always the most enduring relationships any of us will ever have. After all, we may split up with a partner or break up with our friends, but no one can divorce a sibling. Furthermore, these relationships are forged and developed during our formative years, the time when the brain is developing most rapidly, so their effect is profound and becomes deeply embedded in our personality. Such long-lasting, intimate relationships deserve close attention, and they should be used to advantage. They certainly shouldn't be regarded as something to fear, minimise or avoid.

Celebrating sibling relationships

Siblings is unique not only because of my thoroughly positive attitude to sibling relationships. It also differs from other parenting books because I take a long view. Not only will we discuss sibling relationships during your children's early years, but we'll also look both back – to your own childhood – and ahead, to their adulthood and old age. Of course it's vital to know how best to understand and make the most of what's going on when a new baby is born. But what happens later matters too, from the time they start primary school, and onward until they're teenagers, then young adults who are preparing to leave home. Each of these phases presents important opportunities for your children to hone their social and emotional skills and to understand one another better, not least because at each successive stage in their development, they'll have greater cognitive capacity. And throughout their development, I will teach you a number of ways to 'future proof' your children, so you can prepare them to have the best sibling relationships possible when they're adults.

Another special quality of this book is the practical help I offer, based on academic findings and on my own clinical experience. For more than 35 years, I've worked with parents and their families, and watched them overcome every problem imaginable, emerging more competent people, and sharing stronger, more confident bonds. Unlike other parenting books about sibling relationships, you'll be learning about advantages and opportunities rather than focusing only on problems. And that, I believe, is the secret to great sibling relationships.

Instead of preparing yourself to act as referee in a long-running civil war, I hope you'll finish this book feeling as positive as I do about the tremendous advantages your children have when there's more than one child in the family. Instead of worrying about arguments, you'll be eager to help your children learn to solve the issues that arise between them. Instead of imagining a battlefield, you'll consider your home to be the best natural training ground possible for healthy social, emotional and cognitive development.

By the end of this book, you'll know how to encourage each of your children to acquire the incredible gift of emotional sophistication. Best of all, you'll know that the longest relationships they'll ever have will now also be one of the strongest and most enjoyable aspects of their lives.

About the book

In Part 1, you'll learn how the quality of sibling relationships can vary depending on the number of children in your family, their gender and spacing. I'll answer the popular question, 'What's the best number of children to have?' and we'll look at the differences in family dynamics from small through to larger families. You may be considering having a third child but are unsure of the impact on your existing two; you may have three boys and a baby girl and are already seeing signs of jealousy towards the baby; or you may be worrying what's in store for your family with a house full of girls! The information in this section will help you understand your children's behaviour better – in relation to each other and to you as parents. You'll also gain a much better idea about what relationships to expect within your own family.

We'll take a look at sibling relationships in terms of birth order, so you can understand better how children in each birth order position regard the relationships they have with their siblings. When you're able to see things from the viewpoint of each of your children, you'll be better able to understand why conflicts arise, and better able to help each of them develop emotional awareness and good coping strategies. 'Middle child syndrome' is a term bandied about by psychologists – does your middle child show similar traits, and what can you do to alleviate some of their dilemmas? How do you make sure your youngest doesn't get unnecessarily 'babied' by his older siblings? And how can you relieve some of the pressures put on the eldest child, which they may feel too keenly?

Also in the first section, I'll help you understand how your own experiences as a child may be influencing the way you parent your own children now. You may find that by examining your relationship with your own siblings you'll see things you want to emulate, and elements of how you were parented you now wish to change with your own children.

Once we've looked at the make-up of your family, in Part 2 we'll move on to look at the building blocks of a great sibling relationship. This is the core of the book. Here you'll learn how to help your children handle the challenges they'll face as they learn to live productively together. I lay out my building blocks of a good relationship and how you as parents can encourage this with four simple actions.

Then, in the following two sections of the book, we'll take a look at how to apply these building blocks to common situations arising in sibling relationships. Of all the challenges that have been debated in terms of sibling relationships, probably the one cited most often is the introduction of a new baby into the family, and we'll look at this in detail, and work through how best to deal with it. We'll also discuss potential pressure points for siblings at school.

Of course, our sibling relationships don't end when we leave home. If anything, they become more important, especially as we grow older. In Part 3, we'll look at how to maintain good sibling relationships, particularly in later life.

In Part 4, you'll learn simple and practical techniques for when you're faced with a number of specific issues. For each, I will explain the best ways to handle that situation as effectively as possible.

Siblings with special needs, those with chronic illness, those who must endure the loss of a brother or sister, and those for whom a particularly strong ability or talent has been identified present different challenges, and we'll consider these less common circumstances as well. There are also guidelines for what to do if you and your partner separate, or if you have a child who has taken on more responsibility than they can handle easily.

In Part 4 we'll also touch on the single child. Although there are many advantages for those growing up as the only child in their family, there's no natural training ground to help them develop good social and emotional skills when interacting with peers. In this chapter I suggest ways you can help a single child develop a strong and robust EQ.

Throughout this book, you'll notice boxes entitled 'Flashpoint'. These are questions I'm often asked in clinics, and when I speak to parents and teachers in schools. My brief but practical answers to these common questions will, I hope, be directly relevant for many of you.

Psychological advice: is it really based on science?

Before we begin, I want to explain how psychologists arrive at their conclusions, and on what basis they offer advice, so you know how we create guidelines for best parenting practice.

Psychology can't be likened to chemistry or physics or other traditional sciences, for three main reasons. First, when we study the material we need to study – ourselves – we can't step outside ourselves so as to become totally objective. We can't temporarily suspend our human point of view and become suddenly dispassionate. That means that psychological research can't be carried out and analysed as even-handedly as can, for example, the study of light waves. There will always be some inbuilt bias, and this can at times cause us to overlook important information, or to see things in the wrong light.

Second, ethical rules severely limit what we can do when we carry out psychological research. It's absolutely essential that these safeguards are in place when we study human beings (just as they should be when we study other living creatures), but those fierce safeguards limit how much we can conclude from research efforts. For example, if we want to discover the way that learning to read benefits a child, we can't find this out by deliberately denying some children the opportunity to learn to read, while offering to teach that skill to others. We can only choose a benefit – for example, the level of a child's self-confidence – and measure this before and after a child learns to read. We can then suggest – but not know for sure – that the increase in self-confidence that we've found is because the child can now read. In other words, psychologists can note associations between certain measurements – in our example, the ability to read and the child's level of self-confidence – but it's often extremely difficult to prove that the one has caused the other. In our example, it might be that the age when children are able to learn how to read is the same age when a neurological change makes them feel more self-confident. Or perhaps the attention that an adult must give a child in order to teach them to read is what accounts for the increase in self-confidence, rather than the ability to read per se.

And third, because we don't even begin to know yet what exactly makes each of us unique we can't be certain that any result we get when we work with one individual will be the same result we'll get when we work with other individuals, even if we work with them in the same way. Different people may respond differently to our approach. That doesn't mean the approach doesn't work, of course. However, it does mean that we still have to figure out which individuals will be helped by our intervention and which won't respond. That's why progress can be very slow in psychological research. We're so much more complex, and so much more mysterious, than a molecule!

This is also why clinical observation in psychology – that is, looking at what happens when an experienced clinician works with individuals to help them overcome the mental health problems that are troubling them – carries so much more weight in psychology than such an 'anecdotal' approach would carry in other fields of study. Because psychologists can do less 'pure science' – and by that I mean laboratory-based, controlled experiments – it means that clinical experience is a highly valued source of information.

I hope this background information helps you as you read this book. The advice and guidelines you'll be offered throughout are based to some extent on (limited) experimentation, but even more on clinical experience. That means the advice will apply to most of us – but it's important always to remember that there will be exceptions.

You may have picked up this book because your children aren't getting along as you hope they will. Or perhaps you've heard that 'siblings always argue', and you wonder how best to handle the disagreements. If you read what I've written, you'll certainly find out how to ease your worries, and you'll feel you know how to cope better when your children don't seem to be getting on.

But the great thing about this book is that it offers so much more. You'll learn how to solve problems, to be sure – even if they've become well-established bad habits. But you'll also come to see the fantastic opportunities your children have because they're living with others of a similar age. You'll discover how they can learn from each other and acquire interpersonal skills that will set them up for life.

Part 1
The make-up of your family

1

Family size

What is the ideal family size?

How many children should there be in a family to ensure the best sibling relationships? Most parents are desperate to know the answer to this question! My reply is both simple, and easier to achieve than you might think.

The optimum number of children in a family, the number that's most likely to ensure that your family is a happy one, is the number of children you have right now. That's because what matters most in terms of family harmony and happiness – so much so that it swamps all other factors – is your attitude to the family you have.

This is possibly not the answer you were expecting, I know. But just think about it: your positive attitude to your family and your children, and your gratitude for the family you have right now, will permeate your children's attitudes towards each other. If you're looking for something other than what you have now to explain away any problems – 'I think we need another child to "complete" the family', or 'A smaller family would be so much easier' – your children will sense your disquiet. They may even feel they're somehow to blame for your unhappiness.

If, instead, you accept your family as it is, and work with the members you have already, everyone will benefit. You'll all be much happier. And if there are changes in future, your accepting attitude will make it easy for you to adjust to those changes: 'This is what we have now. Let's enjoy it!'

Nonetheless, there will always be differences in how your children will relate to you and to one another that is dependent on how many of them there are.

Before we consider the effects of family size on sibling relationships in more detail, let's take a look at some of the research that's looked at this question, to see if there's anyone who claims to know what the ideal number of children in a family should be.

In 2011, the British parenting website www.bounty.com carried out a large survey to determine what makes for a happy family. They asked 2,116 parents to rate each of their children's behaviour using criteria such as 'ease of care', 'compatibility', 'helps around the house' and 'generally like each other' (this last being a key issue for us). Here's the list the researchers came up with to represent the ideal family size, in decreasing order of happiness according to how the parents surveyed answered the questionnaire:

1. Two girls
2. One boy and one girl
3. Two boys
4. Three girls
5. Three boys
6. Four boys
7. Two girls and one boy
8. Two boys and one girl
9. Three boys and one girl
10. Three girls and one boy
11. Two boys and two girls
12. Four girls.

Where does your family appear on the list? According to the parents in the Bounty survey, two girls is the ideal family constellation. Why did parents rate this combination so highly? The benefits of having two girls, they told the researchers, are that they're 'easy to reason with', 'have very few fights and arguments', 'play nicely together', and 'seem to like each other'. Parents of four girls, on the other hand (rated last, the least ideal family set up), commented that when there are four of them they 'fight and argue all the time', 'are difficult to reason with' and 'create a lot of noise around the house'. Four girls, parents added, also 'rarely confide in us' and 'take ages getting ready for school'.

Is two children, preferably both female, the answer, then? Maybe, but maybe not.

In spring 2015 Eurostat, the Europe-wide statistics agency, published its annual report into happiness across 28 member states, as well as four other states – Switzerland, Iceland, Norway and Serbia. In total, approximately 366,650 individuals were surveyed. Among the many results that emerged from this enormous study, the researchers found that families with *three* or more children are considerably more likely to report that they're 'very happy' than are families with just one or two children. Those with three or more children ranked their happiness as 7.4 out of a possible 11, the highest rating from parents, with 28% claiming to be 'highly happy'.

Across Europe, therefore, it seems that more is better.

If we now move ahead to August 2015 and travel to western Australia, we find the results of another large survey about family size and happiness. Bronwyn Harman, a lecturer in the School of Psychology and Social Science at Edith Cowan University in Perth, spent five years interviewing 950 parents from a wide range of family set-ups – two-parent families, children raised by a single parent, and families where parents identified as LGBT (lesbian, gay, bisexual or transgender). Harman's aim was to discover which families regarded their situation as optimal. She found that the families who scored highest on life satisfaction were those with *four* or more children.

Therefore, in this Australian study, even bigger seems to be better. When Harman asked these parents why they rated their life satisfaction so high, they replied that their joy comes from watching their children interact with and support one another. Children in these larger families, according to their parents, grow up to be independent, socially able, and nurturing, caring individuals. According to these parents, the advantages outweighed disadvantages such as expenses and the limited time parents were able to give to each child.

Three substantial, well-executed and carefully analysed studies, all carried out within the same five years. Three different conclusions. What do we make of this?

What these conflicting conclusions suggest is that no one knows for sure what constitutes the ideal family size – and that's because 'ideal' and 'most satisfying' mean different things to different people. It's also because personal experience colours our perceptions and expectations. In particular, our own experience of childhood – the size of the family in which we grew up and the sibling relationships we knew – will bias our expectations, probably more powerfully than any other factor. If the parents in these surveys had a happy and satisfying family life themselves when they were children, they're very likely to grow up believing that theirs is the ideal family size. If they were unhappy, they're likely to avoid replicating their childhood family constellation.

I hope that you now feel totally entitled to conclude that the number of children you have is the best number possible. If you truly believe this, your children will be happy, and they'll feel fortunate to be part of an 'ideal' family.

That said, it's helpful to observe what happens in different family set-ups, because families of different sizes encourage different sorts of sibling relationships.

Let's take a look at the advantages and disadvantages of having different numbers of children in a family, so you'll know how to capitalise on the positives, and at the same time, will be forewarned and prepared for the problems you're likely to encounter.

You may recognise many of the patterns I'm about to describe in your own family, although of course none of them will mirror your situation exactly. That's because each family – and each child, for that matter – is unique. These are general patterns, based on research as well as clinical experience. The secret is to use them as templates and adjust them to fit your own circumstances.

Families with two children

In smaller families, parents have more time to spend with each child, so their impact as a role model will be greater than it will be for parents who have more children. The child who gains most from this is the firstborn, who has the luxury of enjoying exclusive parental attention before their sibling arrives. The downside is that they find themselves having to adjust to decreased parental input as they gain a sibling.

With only two children to look after, parents have the time to explain to each of them how best to solve problems. They'll have the opportunities to show each by example as well as by instruction how to generate lots of possible solutions and listen calmly to those who disagree. They'll also have relatively more opportunities to demonstrate to quarrelling children the benefits of learning to compromise.

This relatively luxurious allocation of time means that children will also have more time to talk with their parents generally. As a result, they'll be exposed to – and therefore learn to use – language that's more sophisticated and nuanced than will children who spend time mainly with their peers. This in turn makes it possible for them to express their needs clearly and articulately from an early age. Children in smaller families tend to do better academically, therefore, because they've had more sophisticated linguistic input – although it's important to add that this will be tempered by their parents' level of education.

On the other hand, research has made it abundantly clear that linguistic ability and IQ, although important, are by no means the only skills a child needs in order to have the best chance of getting what they want and need in life. Good social skills are also vital, in particular knowing how to make themselves likeable to other children while at the same time knowing how to appeal to adults without antagonising their peers. Here, children in smaller families are at a disadvantage, because these 'street skills' can only be learned by spending a fair amount of unchaperoned time with as wide a variety of other children as possible.

What sort of sibling relationship is most likely to develop, then, when there are two children?

Sibling rivalry and competition is likely to be more intense, because each child is competing with only one other individual. Therefore, whenever they feel aggrieved, all their anger is directed on the only target – their one sibling. Fortunately, any aggression they show to that sibling, particularly if they're girls and the age gap between them is relatively large, is likely to be more verbal than physical. This is partly because children in smaller families tend to have a broader vocabulary – more accurate weapons in this armoury, if you will – and partly because they know they're more likely to get caught if they lash out physically at their sibling, because parents who have fewer children to look after are more likely to notice this sort of socially unacceptable behaviour. They can hide verbal aggression more easily as well – snide remarks are easier to deny than scratches or bruises.

Technically, each child in a small family should feel less deprived of parental attention than those who have to share that attention with more brothers and sisters. Unfortunately, however, it's often the case that when there are only two children, they may not feel that way. Perhaps this is because the more there is of something, the more each of us expects and wants to have of it. Whatever the reason, children in smaller families recall more readily the occasions when they felt short-changed of parental attention.

Sometimes, when children are caught out, they'll unite rather than compete. It's not unusual, particularly in families where there are two children, for one of them, usually the elder, to encourage the other to be the one who pushes parental limits; for example, to break a particular house rule. If they're caught, however, rather than the younger one feeling aggrieved because their sibling got them into trouble, they'll come together to share their sense of injustice – especially if their parents reprimanded both of them. Rather than competing for parental attention, what they both wanted at that moment was to avoid it. The tendency, therefore, is to turn to one another to commiserate, and to unite against the 'common enemy' – in this case, their parents!

What is the course of a sibling relationship in smaller families in the longer term? The likelihood is that they'll remain close to one another throughout their lives. You may be wondering how it's possible, in a relationship that's bound to be as intense – and oftentimes, as antagonistic – as it is when two children grow up together, how this could possibly be the case. The reason is that it's the intensity of emotion rather than its 'colour' that counts when it comes to determining the strength of a relationship.

It seems that when we experience any intense emotion towards another person, it causes us to feel close to them, and this will be the case whether the experience we shared was primarily negative or more positive. Think, at the very extreme end of the scale, of the Stockholm syndrome. This is a psychological condition in which hostages develop strong positive feelings for their captors, presumably as a survival strategy during their captivity.

A strong bond in adulthood between two siblings is even more likely if the children are close in age and of the same gender, as you will learn in the next chapter.

> ## FLASHPOINT
>
> *I'm feeling so guilty. I just can't give my second child the same undivided attention that I managed to give my firstborn. Is this OK, or should we be doing something to compensate?*
>
> Each child in a family has their own 'built-in' compensations as a consequence of their birth order position. Your eldest received that extra attention from you, so their linguistic skills and cognitive development enjoyed a great start. But your second child will find it easier than their older sibling to share with others and to come up with compromises when there are disagreements – and will, therefore, find it easy to be liked by their peers – because they came into a world where this was necessary from the beginning.
>
> That said, one of the most enjoyable – and for your children, fondly remembered – things you can do is to carve out a regular 'special outing' with each of your children. For example, take each one out for a meal on their own with you once a month, or offer each one a treat you know they'll love, such as a trip to the zoo or to see a film. What you do and how often you manage to do it are less important than making sure you do something regularly, that you stick to your promise, and that while you are on your adventure together you focus entirely on the child who's with you at that time.

Families with three children

As family size increases, the amount of time parents can spend exclusively with each child decreases. This is correlated with lower verbal ability and IQ scores (although the correlation is often not significant), and of course it depends on other factors as well, such as the educational opportunities each child is offered. This association is also tempered by the age difference between the first child and subsequent children. A firstborn, remember, enjoys a period of time exclusively with their parents, no matter how many siblings follow, and this exclusive time occurs during a critical phase in their cognitive and linguistic development. They will, therefore, reap the same benefits as will firstborns in all other family constellations.

If the firstborn in a larger family is a good deal older than their siblings (at least four years), younger children will benefit, because the older child becomes another verbal role model in the family, someone who can enrich the vocabulary of their siblings by their example. At times, an older sibling may be even more influential than a parent in this regard. Piaget, the Swiss child psychologist who taught us so much about children's cognitive development, maintained that a child learns more from someone who is only slightly more cognitively mature than they are than they will from someone (an adult) whose development is well beyond that of the child. Furthermore, the 'lingo' younger children learn from an older sibling is likely to be more appropriate than the terms parents use, when children talk to their peers.

Good social skills are paramount for the developing child, contributing to their ability to get what they want and to communicate and negotiate effectively. When we consider the development of good social skills, research suggests that children in families where there are three or more rather than just two are at an advantage. Each child has, not one, but two competitors, each with a different personality and a different way of coping. As a result, they become more adaptable. They have to learn a number of different ways to get along, and they have to perfect a number of strategies to ensure that they get what they want, because they're interacting (and competing) with more people.

Children in families where there are three are, therefore, more socially skilled. Their vocabulary may be slightly less advanced than it is for children from smaller families, but their ability to speak the language of their peers will be better.

More specifically, then, what's the relationship like between siblings when there are three children?

First, the rivalry between them is likely to be slightly less intense than it is when there are only two of them. This is because the majority of children in a three-child family – two out of the three – come into the world expecting to share from the moment they're born. They'll accept sharing as the norm, and they won't feel aggrieved that each receives less one-to-one attention from parents. Of course, the firstborn still feels the loss of exclusive parental attention, just as all firstborns do. You'll learn more about this in Chapter 4 on birth order and Chapter 10 in Part 3. The second- and third-born children will, however, accept less parental attention relatively easily. This will be particularly so if the firstborn is substantially older than subsequent children, because the eldest can help nurture younger ones, although when it comes to understanding sibling relationships, there are always complications! The level and intensity of sibling rivalry also depends on the temperament of each child. We'll look at this complicating factor in Chapter 3.

The level of aggression is also different in larger families. When there are three, the type of aggression one sibling may show towards another is less predictable than when there are only two. If all three are girls, and if their parents – particularly mum, their gender role model – is generally calm and cooperative, they're more likely to compete verbally than resort to physical aggression. If all three are boys, however, their behaviour will depend largely on their verbal agility, and on how their father – their gender role model – behaves. They'll be more likely to talk through disagreements than to use physical aggression if their vocabulary is well developed, and if their father behaves calmly and approaches challenges logically rather than emotionally. Age also matters. Children in a three-child family, whatever their gender, are more likely to use physical rather than verbal means to sort out disagreements with their siblings when they're very young, particularly if their vocabulary is limited and if at least one of them is impulsive.

Finally, there's the potential problem of 'uneven numbers' when there are three rather than two children. If two of them get along better with one another than they do with the third, either because they're the same gender, are similar in age or are compatible in temperament, then unfortunately it's quite likely that two of them will gang up on the outsider. This can be difficult to manage and parents often make the mistake of feeling kinder and more sympathetic towards the child who's left out. When that happens, the other two only become more jealous and more aggressive towards the third. This problem is discussed in Part 3, Chapter 12, where you'll learn how best to deal with ganging up and bullying.

Families with four or more children

The biggest issue in large families is the allocation of parental time. The more children there are in the family, the less time parents have to spend with each of them. As a consequence, children in large families have fewer opportunities to hear mature language and to observe adults as they solve problems in a sophisticated and logical way. On the other hand, however (as we've already seen in families where there are three children), the younger siblings benefit hugely because they'll be introduced to peer-appropriate terminology by their older siblings. Older children who enjoy teaching will also impart some problem-solving techniques to their younger siblings.

You might think that, with so few opportunities to enjoy exclusive parental attention, the rivalry among siblings in large families would be more intense. This isn't usually the case, because two factors work against it. First, everyone except the firstborn has always shared parental time and attention with other children. All of them – again, except the firstborn – are used to sharing adult attention. Because they've never expected to receive exclusive parental attention, they don't feel resentful that they aren't offered it.

Second, older children learn quite quickly that if they help their parents nurture their younger brothers and sisters, their parents praise them and pay attention to them, and may even feel that they don't need to lavish so much time on the younger ones. If, however, the older children are aggressive towards the little ones, parents are likely to turn their attention to the child who's been attacked; so when the older ones are aggressive, they lose out. Therefore, the eldest child quickly learns that a kind and caring attitude towards their younger siblings yields better results than expressing their jealousy. There's an added benefit, too – those who nurture feel good simply because they've behaved altrusitically. Research has shown that when we help someone else, it triggers the release of oxytocin, making us feel warmer towards others and more positively connected with them.

When there is competitive behaviour in large families, the form it takes depends mainly on who's doing the arguing. Younger children, as well as children of any age who are more impulsive by nature, are more likely to resort to physical means. Unfortunately, this is particularly likely if they've witnessed this sort of approach among older members of the family. On the other hand, children who are more privy to verbal arguments will themselves resort to words to sort out differences. When there's a big age gap between them, younger children are most likely to defend themselves by calling for help, because they know their parents and older siblings are likely to come to their rescue. One of my children's teachers once remarked that the youngest child's most powerful weapon is a single word: 'Mum!'

Finally, an interesting and common phenomenon in large families is to break themselves into smaller groups, to form 'sub-families'. Two or sometimes three children will form a close and cooperative bond. They'll stick together and rarely fight among themselves. As you might expect, siblings close in age are *less* likely to make such bonds, particularly if they're the same gender. Because they're likely to want many of the same things from their parents, they'll be more competitive than affiliative, at least when they're young. These subdivisions work well within families, but can lead to division if not all children are included in a sub-family.

FLASHPOINT

Two of my children tend to 'gang up' against my little son. They can be really cliquey and leave him out of games. What can I do about this?

Before you step in, step back! Are you sure your 'left-out' child really wants to join in with his siblings' games? Is he close in age? Are his interests similar? And most important of all, are you reacting to *this* situation, or are you identifying with the left-out child because that's what happened to you, and you're forgetting that this situation isn't necessarily the same as your own childhood experience? Try to look at what's going on from *their* perspective.

If the left-out child really does feel left out, your best approach is to suggest that the pair who play together come up with a game suitable for all three of them, and play it some of the time. Then reward the two of them for inviting their brother to join them, rather than focusing your attention on the left-out child. Meanwhile, ask your third child if he'd like to invite a friend over to play, and try to make this happen as often as you can. This approach allows the pair to feel powerful because they can help their brother and when they aren't doing so their brother isn't feeling left out because he has his own friend to play with.

If you discover that the left-out child is actually not bothered about being left out – perhaps he's even relieved – then simply make sure that all three of them, the pair and the one, are able to play the games they've chosen or pursue the activities that suit them best. After all, siblings rarely enjoy identical interests, and each child will differ temperamentally – particularly in terms of how much socialising is enough for each of them.

When children in large families are growing up, the closest bonds are often between those more widely spaced in age, one acting as the caring child and the other as the cared-for child. In adulthood, however, siblings who have shared more emotional experiences – even, as we've already learned, if those experiences consisted primarily of arguments – are more likely to remain close to one another, whatever their age gap. So, for example, the close-in-age brothers who didn't have much to do with each other growing up, who often clashed and who spent time with different friends, often enjoy a close relationship in adulthood as they reminisce about their parents' approach to discipline, and other shared memories.

In summary, despite the many disadvantages of large families – the lack of parental time, relatively fewer opportunities to learn from adults, and probably fewer material resources available for each individual – the compensations are many. There are numerous opportunities to learn different ways of behaving: as a giver, a receiver, a comforter, a teacher.

In a larger family, the focus is taken away from the parents because the other siblings also play an important role in shaping relationships as well as cognitive and social skills.

When there are a number of children in the family, they'll be forced to negotiate and compromise in the face of fewer resources, and therefore become more innovative. Their greater social skills and their adaptability will serve them well throughout their lives. Finally, children in large families are likely always to have someone they can call on. They'll be able to obtain different sorts of help and advice because of the variety of talent all around them. This is a resource they'll have for the rest of their lives, and it's one that's more useful and more precious than any amount of material goods.

Summary

The number of children you choose to have will affect the relationships they form with one another. In smaller families, rivalry and competition predominate, whereas in larger families there will be more cooperation and caretaking behaviours. In the longer term, however, the closeness of the bonds between siblings, however many sisters and brothers they have, will be determined not just by family size, but also by a number of mediating factors, including the spacing between your children, their gender differences and, most important of all, on your input and attitudes.

Let's turn now to these other factors.

2

Gender and spacing

You now know how the size of your family helps to determine the way your children are likely to interact with one another.

But that's only a start. You'll be even better able to predict the tenor and course of their relationships if you add in the effects of gender and of the age gaps between them.

Let's consider, then, how these two important factors influence the way your children will relate to one another, and how they affect the level and intensity of sibling rivalry.

Effects of spacing on sibling relationships

When psychologists study the age gaps between siblings and the effect this has on the intensity of sibling rivalry, the most powerful influencing factor they find is parental expectations. In other words, as with family size, it's your attitude towards that spacing that matters most. If you decide that the age gap between your children is the best one possible – no matter what that spacing looks like – then as far as your children are concerned, it will be. Remember, your children are more sensitive to how you're feeling than they are to anything else in their environment. Your attitude and outlook have immense power. If they sense that you're pleased with the family constellation, they'll feel calmer and less threatened, and therefore less likely to consider their sibling to be a threat to their wellbeing.

Your attitude to the age gaps is so critical that I would urge you to make that your primary consideration when you're thinking about the spacing between your children. In a moment I'll point out the pros and cons of different age gaps so you can be best informed if you've not yet had all the children you plan to have. Remember, however, that none of these facts is as important as the way you regard your family – even if you can't come up with a good reason why you feel this way! Your attitude is more powerful than any other factor. Bear this in mind, too, if you're already pregnant with your next child, even if the spacing isn't exactly what you'd hoped or planned. You can still make it work, simply by deciding that it *will* work for you and for your other children.

To help you capitalise on the assets of various age gaps, and to be forewarned about the potential problems, let's now consider the various possibilities.

Closely spaced siblings (an age gap of two years or less)

This gap is the hardest on you physically. If you become pregnant again quite soon after giving birth, your body is unlikely to have fully recovered from the previous experience, so you'll feel quite exhausted, more so than if you were caring for your young child without having to cope with this physical challenge at the same time. This is particularly true during the late stages of pregnancy, when as you know it's difficult to sleep restfully. It's hard enough to remain calm and rational, and to deal effectively with the challenges you inevitably face when you're dealing with a baby or toddler. However, when your body is changing and you're short of sleep, even small problems can feel insurmountable. Having two babies close together is, therefore, asking a lot of yourself.

It will take a great deal of stamina to cope with someone who's unlikely to be sleeping through the night yet, and probably isn't toilet trained. Your little one will still need help with the basics – dressing and feeding – and they'll want you to entertain them constantly. To complicate matters further, you can't rely on rational explanation to

2 Gender and spacing

soothe a young child when they're upset, because as yet they have little impulse control, and they're still too young to understand the consequences of many of their actions.

That said, once the new baby arrives, very quickly the needs of these two will become relatively similar, so it won't take long for you to learn to care for both of them effectively and efficiently.

There is a cost, however. The only way you can do this is to treat them similarly. That's fine in terms of their physical care. However, it means that oftentimes you'll miss the chance to enjoy the individuality of each child, and, indirectly, this has the unfortunate consequence of increasing the rivalry between them. Why?

Each child in a family wants more than anything else to be considered unique and special. The more parents can emphasise the differences between their children, the less each will feel the need to distinguish themselves, and outshine their siblings, particularly in those areas where you are treating your children as equivalent. Therefore, although it's easier to treat two closely spaced children alike, it may well have the effect of increasing your workload, because you'll have to deal with more aggressive outbursts and more competitive behaviour than you will if you praise and care for each child in ways that reward their individual differences.

Two children who are closely spaced are also likely to cost more in the short term, because they'll need much of the same equipment, particularly if and when they're of similar size. That means you're going to have to purchase – or, if you're lucky, borrow – two sets of most things, rather than being able to rely on handing down clothing, prams, highchairs and the like from one child to the next.

Later on, on the other hand, because they'll share so many interests and are likely to be of similar ability in many ways, they'll probably enjoy the same sorts of outings and holidays. This may or may not save money, but it will definitely reduce the amount of time you have to spend planning schedules and taking them to their various activities.

Another big advantage of close spacing is that although this period of total caring will be incredibly intense at the outset when you have two who are close in age and similar in needs, your reward comes sooner. You're likely to enjoy a return to a more normal life – unbroken nights and a more predictable schedule – sooner than you would if you space your children more widely. You can also count on them being at the same school for long periods of time, thus minimising the need to arrange drop-offs at different schools. All this means that you'll be feeling calmer and more in control sooner. Your more relaxed attitude will of course mean that the children will also feel calmer and happier, and, as a result, less likely to irritate one another and end up arguing.

Furthermore, close spacing means your children will accept one another's presence more readily. This is especially true for the older child, who is unlikely to remember that there was ever a period when they enjoyed your exclusive attention.

At the same time, however, they're likely to compete for the same toys, and they'll try to outperform one another in a bid for your attention. Initially, therefore, they'll be intensely rivalrous; but even this has its saving grace. As you know, strong emotions – whatever their colour – lead to a feeling of closeness later. The likelihood of a close bond is even greater because, being at a similar level of development, they'll grow up with a similar understanding of the experiences they share. All this means they're likely to form a very close bond in the long run.

In summary, if you want to minimise total dependency time, and if you feel up to the physical challenge, having two children close together should work well for you and for your children. The sort of relationship you'll be dealing with when there's a close age gap is fiery – lots of competition for you to meet their (similar) needs, to treat them as individuals, and to pay attention to them, very often at the same time, particularly during the first few years. (We'll look at how to deal with these issues in Part 2 of the book.) On the other hand, because the older child will still be so young when their sibling comes into the family, they'll feel less displaced than they would if the age gap were larger; in effect, it will seem to them both as if they've always been together. Finally, a long-term payoff is that two closely spaced children are likely to enjoy a strong lifelong bond because they'll have been through so much together.

Moderately spaced siblings (a two- to four-year age gap)

It takes most women approximately 18 months to two years before they feel fully recovered after giving birth. Not long after this, your child – now a pre-schooler – is more likely to be sleeping through the night, so that will also help you to feel more rested.

Your child is probably also able to feed themselves and get dressed on their own – at least to some extent – and perhaps they'll even be toilet trained. All this allows you to feel stronger and more like 'yourself' again, ready to deal more rationally and calmly with the jealousy your older child is bound to feel when the new baby arrives.

And therein lies the catch. Your older child will have become used to your exclusive attention. They'll be acutely aware of the huge changes that take place when the baby arrives. They're bound to feel threatened by this new arrival, primarily because they are aware that they're no longer the centre of your attention.

Although you may think you can talk things through with your older child rationally, their ability to imagine the future is not yet well established. Therefore, no matter how hard you have tried to prepare them, it will still come as a terrible shock to them once you bring home this needy, helpless little bundle. Pre-schoolers are at the maximum 'why' stage, so they're likely to ask you repeatedly – and anxiously – why you aren't spending as much time with them now, and why this baby has to remain in the house.

Not only is the older child's sense of the future still underdeveloped, their ability to 'decentre' – to see things from other people's points of view – is still quite fragile as well. This means that any attempt you make to describe the joy this baby will bring to you all, or how great it will be in the future when they can play with the new arrival, is unlikely to mean much to them at this point. All they can see is that you're now spending large chunks of time with the new baby instead of with them. The result? Almost certainly your once-calm, cheerful older child will become angry, frustrated and increasingly demanding. Even though you resolve to ignore this negative behaviour, at some point you're likely to feel you can't take any more of it. That's when you turn your attention to your older child, and no matter whether you show kindness and understanding or you become cross and irritated, that attention will have the unfortunate consequence of reinforcing your unhappy child's negative attention-seeking behaviours.

Therefore, although the upside of spacing your children two to four years apart is that this longer gap means you'll be better able to deal with their different needs, it won't always work that way. Your older child doesn't need you to feed them or change them, but they're still hungry for your attention. In many ways, there will be times when you feel they're at least as demanding as the baby. Unfortunately, this is likely to be whenever the baby needs you most, because that's when the older child feels most overlooked.

With closely spaced children, it's all about having the stamina to meet the similar demands of two children simultaneously. When the spacing is a bit wider, you still have to cope with those simultaneous demands, but now the needs are different, so you can't 'double up' when responding to the two of them.

As you can probably tell, I don't think a two- to four-year age gap is a very easy one for parents, and I don't understand why so many childcare experts recommend it. True, you're now physically stronger than if you'd become pregnant again almost straight away. However, the distress you'll have to deal with in your older child demands you to be in full possession of a huge store of energy, a forgiving nature, and incredible amounts of patience. No matter how hard you try, you won't be able to make the older child understand that this is just a temporary situation. Whatever you say, they're simply not cognitively sophisticated enough to realise that one day this baby will become a companion, and that the fun they'll have together will be well worth the temporary lack of attention now.

There is, however, one enormous compensation if you choose this age gap, and that is that your older child will probably be in nursery school by the time you give birth again. Therefore, at least when the older child is away, you can enjoy the opportunity to focus exclusively on your new baby without worrying about the jealous feelings your behaviour is likely to create.

It's important to bear in mind your children's very differing needs whenever someone else is around and offers to help you out. Most mothers' initial reaction is to ask them to look after their older child. In fact, it would be far better to ask for help with the baby. That will free you to spend some one-to-one time with your pre-schooler, time that will go a long way towards relieving resentment and rivalrous feelings and establishing the foundations of a positive bond.

From the children's point of view, I think you can now see that this is the age gap that most encourages sibling rivalry, particularly during the first three or four years, and particularly from the older child's viewpoint.

Once they're both in school, however, you'll start to reap the benefits of a two- to four-year age gap. The difference between their abilities will have decreased, and they will begin to share a number of similar interests. By now, your younger one is likely to start looking up to her older sibling as well, so the older one, instead of feeling jealous and overlooked, will enjoy a bit of hero worship. She'll start to feel like a ground-breaker and the little one's protector.

As you no doubt remember from the first chapter, closeness develops whether the initial interactions between children are intensely positive or intensely negative. Nevertheless, from your point of view as referee and rule maker, it's much easier when the interactions are cooperative and positive rather than antagonistic and aggressive.

In summary, a two- to four-year age gap is advantageous because it allows you time to become fully fit again before your next pregnancy. However, you'll need to be on top form, because that age difference also means that you'll be dealing with a great deal of jealousy and quite intense sibling rivalry in the early years.

Widely spaced siblings (a four-year or longer age gap)

You could almost think of four years as a 'mini-generational' gap because, at least in the early years, your children's needs will hardly overlap. Furthermore, by the time your next child is born, the older one will be in school at least part-time if not all day. That means you'll have generous amounts of time to focus fully on the new baby while the older child is at school, thus sparing the older one feelings of jealousy. At the same time, because you'll be an experienced mother, you'll have a better chance of timing the baby's feeds and naps so that you can maximise after-school time with your older child.

By the age of four to five, a child has become quite cognitively sophisticated, better able to understand now that you're not deliberately excluding her or showing a preference for the baby when you pay attention to the little one. In particular, a four-year-old is becoming able to decentre – that is, to see the world from other people's points of view and to appreciate that they may be different from her own. That allows her to understand both the baby's helplessness and your need to find ways to care for two, much more so than she could have done only a year or so earlier.

As I'm sure you've guessed already, a larger age gap allows you to meet the needs of both children more easily than when they're of a more similar age. As a result, rivalrous and competitive feelings will be minimised, so you won't need to spend as much time being a peacekeeper.

The sort of relationship they'll develop is also quite different than it is when the children are close in age. An older child will be more interested in than jealous of the new arrival, and with their more advanced cognitive skills they'll soon learn that offers of help are the best way to receive positive attention from their parents. Thus the older child learns how to care for others under the watchful eyes of their parents. They also learn that caring for others is rewarding – both extrinsically, in terms of parental praise, and intrinsically. That's because when we nurture someone else, the brain releases oxytocin, which makes us feel safe and secure.

The baby benefits from the extra attention as well, of course. The added linguistic input promotes language development. The new arrival will also learn to accept care from more than one source, something that makes it easier for them later on, when they may have to adjust to new situations.

The two of them will develop a close bond, but not as equal companions. Instead, this bond is best characterised as 'carer and cared-for'. The younger child will look up to and admire their older sibling, and will later rely on them for support and guidance. The older child will feel protective towards their younger sibling.

They may not, however, share as many interests and therefore as many adventures together, and as a result they may be less close as teenagers and young adults than siblings who are very close in age.

This age gap is beneficial for both children. However, it can go wrong. There may be circumstances when the older child becomes overly responsible, and starts to feel anxious, resentful and over-protective. I'll explain how to avoid this situation, or – if it has already arisen – how to sort things out, in Part 3.

Effects of gender on sibling relationships

The notion of gender is changing even as I write this.

Never before have we known such a seismic shift in the way we think of gender. Until fairly recently, there were two categories of gender, just as there were two categories of sex. In order to understand better what's currently happening now, and how it's affecting relationships between siblings, let me start by defining these two terms.

Our sex, categorised as either female or male, is determined by biological differences. These are our anatomical differences – whether we have a vagina or a penis, for example – and our physiological differences, the relative amounts of testosterone, oestrogen and progesterone we have circulating in our body. Our sex is determined by genetics, our DNA. Males have 46 chromosomes plus an X and a Y chromosome; females have 46 plus two X chromosomes.

We tend to think of sex as binary and clear-cut, but in truth that's not the case as often as you might imagine. Some men have two or even three X chromosomes, whereas some women have a Y chromosome. Genitalia, too, may be mixed. When this occurs – estimates are that between 0.015% and 1.7% of the population fall into this category – it may not even be at all clear when the baby is born whether it is male or female. As a result, a sex is simply assigned to the baby.

Gender is something quite different from sex. Gender is determined not biologically, but socially and culturally. It can vary from society to society, and it may change across time.

Take, for example, the current belief that pink is a girl's colour and blue is for boys. This is actually an extremely recent idea. In 1918, for example, the trade publication *Earnshaw's Infants' Department* published an article about 'appropriate' colours for boys and girls. Here's an excerpt: 'The generally accepted rule is pink for the boys and blue for the girls. The reason is that pink, being a more decided and a stronger color, is more suitable for the boy while blue, which is more delicate and dainty, is prettier for the girl.'

It was only in the 1940s that manufacturers, for no empirically based reason, seem arbitrarily to have decided to reverse this notion. Nowadays, we almost always think pink is a girl's colour and blue the colour for boys.

Another good example of how gender stereotypes change is when we consider high-heeled shoes. High heels were initially designed not for women at all, but for upper-class men to wear when they were hunting on horseback. Over time, women began to wear high heels as well. In compensation – to distinguish their footwear – men's heels became shorter and fatter, while women's shoes were designed with ever higher and thinner heels.

Back, then, to gender development. A baby's gender is generally assigned by carers when the baby is born, and in most cases it simply follows in line with sexual characteristics. Gender identity then evolves according to family interactions, as well as being influenced by what the individual learns from peers, at school and from wider society.

Today, however, a growing number of adolescents and adults, and even some children, no longer accept what they're told by these outside sources. Instead, they feel freer now to question their assigned gender identity. What has allowed for this increased freedom isn't clear, but it is now increasingly acceptable to question one's gender identity. To complicate matters, there are a growing number of categories from which we may choose our gender. The most up-to-date list I found at the time of writing contained 47 terms for gender! Some examples include: aromantic, asexual, bigender, demisexual, gay, genderqueer, lesbian, metrosexual and pansexual.

What effect does this emerging new concept of gender have on the relationship between siblings? During the early years, not a lot. Very young children – most children under school age – tend to categorise most things in binary, or black and white, terms. It's also extremely unusual for a pre-schooler to be able to hold two contradictory concepts about the same thing at the same time. Therefore, for most very young children, sex and gender will be one and the same; either male or female, boy or girl. They will identify with and imitate other people, particularly carers and older siblings, whose sex/gender assignment they believe matches their own, and they will begin to define themselves as either male or female.

If the age gap between two children is wide – more than four years – the younger one will look up to and imitate their older sibling if they perceive that sibling to share their same gender identity. If their gender identities differ, they're likely to accentuate those differences so as to be seen as unique to their parents and therefore worthy of special attention.

If the age gap between two siblings is small, then the more strongly each identifies with the same gender/sex, the more openly rivalrous they'll be, each competing with the other to be most noticed by parents. That's why when children are young, two brothers or two sisters will be more rivalrous and competitive than will a brother and a sister, because of course the latter pair can distinguish themselves more easily in their parents' eyes by their gender.

Sometime between the ages of four and seven, however, children become able to consider that there can be a number of sub-categories within any larger category. They also gradually become more able to hold different ideas about the same thing. These cognitive abilities grow and strengthen until, by the time they're adolescents, most young people feel comfortable considering and accepting the existence of multiple sub-categories and numerous conflicting points of view. It is at this point that they may begin seriously to question their gender identity.

What this will do to sibling relationships is too new for me to say. My guess is that in families where it's acceptable to question sensitive and incredibly complicated issues such as gender identity, sibling relationships are likely to be strengthened. This is because siblings may decide to talk about these issues together before discussing them with parents. Children are often more comfortable talking through the possibility of enormous change with someone similar in age before broaching the topic with a parent.

What will happen in families where deviation from traditional roles would be frowned upon is more complicated. On the one hand, the child who is questioning their gender may feel drawn to a sibling who identifies as that child would like to identify, so the two of them may become closer. If the child who's questioning gender is now feeling different from a sibling who previously shared the same gender identity, that child may now feel less competitive with their sibling, happy to co-exist without a fight, because they feel more distinct from the other. My guess is that they'll become less rivalrous but probably also less close.

These are some possibilities, but at this point we can only speculate.

Intriguing as it is to think about how the evolving definition of gender may affect sibling relationships, at present the vast majority of children see themselves as either male or female, and their sex and gender as one and the same. What can be said about the effect on sibling relationships for these children (the vast majority) who accept the traditional definition of gender? There are two main effects, and it's interesting to note that they contradict one another.

First, sibling pairs who are the same gender will, particularly when they're close in age, feel much more rivalrous during their early years than will sibling pairs who are of different genders. This is, as you know, because two siblings with different genders can use this difference to appear special to their parents and therefore gain their attention. At the same time, sibling pairs of the same gender, although rivalrous when young, are likely to identify with one another increasingly as they mature, and they will therefore form a close and supportive bond later on.

FLASHPOINT

How can I try to reduce the intense rivalry between my two daughters?

The secret here is to look out for the differences between the two of them, and whenever you can do so sincerely, to praise and encourage those differences. For example, say both of your daughters are unusually athletic and well coordinated. The elder, however, is more strongly built than her sister and is also keenly competitive, whereas her sister loves music, is less competitive, and is more delicately built.

You could try introducing the elder to competitive swimming. That way, she'd have the chance not only to use her strength and sense of competition, she'll also learn to behave as a team member. This last advantage will teach her cooperative skills that hopefully will transfer to her relationship with her sister.

Meanwhile, you could offer her sister dancing lessons. This gives her the opportunity to use her athleticism as well as her love of music – and, of course, dancing allows her to earn your praise for something she loves doing but that is different from her sister's talents.

In families where the age gaps are wide and where gender roles are traditional, it's very likely that a caring/cared-for relationship will develop between the elder and the younger sibling. This is particularly likely to happen when the elder of the siblings is female, because our society still encourages the gender stereotype that females are the carers.

Second, it's interesting to note that in larger families, the gender-specific characteristics of the majority tend to predominate. In other words, when there are more males than females in the family, the females tend to be more tomboyish. They also generally find it easier to get on with their brothers, and with boys generally. When there are more females, the males are often described as more understanding by their sisters, and are likely to be seen as more nurturing than males who've not grown up with sisters. A related observation is that in large families where all the children are of the same gender, they tend to exhibit behaviours and preferences that could be described as almost caricatures of that gender – very 'girly' females in all-girl families, and extremely 'macho' males in families where everyone identifies as a boy.

FLASHPOINT

What happens to the family dynamic when we have three girls and one boy?

Some fairly predictable tendencies arise under these circumstances, although how they manifest themselves depends on how parents treat the child of the other gender. If that child is treated as more 'special' than the others – say, for example, that after three girls, a longed-for boy is born – the other siblings are likely to bond closely with one another, and tease or in other ways ostracise the 'special' child, because they'll feel jealous of the extra fond attention that child receives.

If, on the other hand, parents welcome the difference of the one, but do not at the same time give that child extra privileges and attention, the bonds between the siblings will be determined as in any other family, by age gap and compatible personality characteristics. It must be added, however, that when the youngest is the only boy or the only girl, and not overly favoured by their parents, the older siblings often feel fond of and protective towards the youngest, and tend to encourage that child's gender-specific differences.

Summary

In this chapter we've examined the extraordinary complexity that makes for relationships between your children. Their relationships are dependent not only on how many of them are in the family, but also on the age gaps between them, as well as on their gender. This last, gender, has become one of the most complex characteristics that humans use to determine our identity.

And all this before we add in the effects of individual personalities and of how parents respond to their children!

3

Temperament

Each of your children, even if you have identical twins, will have his or her own unique personality, and unfortunately there's no guarantee that it will mesh beautifully with the other personalities in your family. This will be true not only among your children, but also regarding your own relationship with each child.

Although love, being measureless, is something we feel equally for all our children, you will almost certainly find that it will be easier to get along with some of your offspring than it will with others. The children will feel the same way, both about you and their siblings.

It will be helpful, therefore, for you to learn as much as you can about character; and, in particular, which traits are more heavily genetically loaded and which have been primarily learned. You'll need to accept and work with those qualities that are genetically loaded. On the other hand, those traits that are more the result of learning than of genetics – and these are the vast majority – are ones your child can learn to change, or at least learn to curb when appropriate.

Knowing the origins of the many aspects of your child's character will allow you to understand which aspects to work with, and which traits you can help your child change when necessary. It means you'll be in the best position to help your children resolve disputes realistically and successfully and to develop the best bonds possible, despite – or perhaps because of – the differences in their personalities.

Theories about personality: then and now

We tend to think of personality measurement as a fairly recent development. However, physicians and philosophers have attempted to categorise individuals according to their character for thousands of years. The Greek scholar Hippocrates was the first to incorporate the idea of human 'temperament' into his medical theories. Drawing from even earlier ideas from Egypt and Mesopotamia, Hippocrates suggested that the relative composition of four of our bodily fluids – blood, yellow bile, black bile and phlegm – determine which of four temperaments would be dominant for each of us. Hippocrates' four temperaments were:

- *Sanguine:* Optimistic, sociable
- *Choleric:* Irritable, short-tempered
- *Melancholic:* Quiet, analytical
- *Phlegmatic:* Relaxed, peaceful.

He assumed that these types remain relatively stable throughout an individual's lifetime. This idea has been accepted without question until very recently.

At the end of the nineteenth century, the British doctor and mathematician Sir Frances Galton suggested that we could create a more exact and comprehensive list of human personality traits by gathering together all the possible personality-related adjectives in the English language. In 1936, Gordon Allport, a professor in the sociology department at Harvard University, decided to put Galton's suggestion into practice. He created a list of over 4,000 adjectives that he believed included all possible human personality traits.

Not long afterwards, the British academic Raymond Cattell used factor analysis, a statistical tool popular with social scientists at the time, to reduce this unwieldy list to 16 key personality factors. Cattell's list includes characteristics such as warmth, social boldness, tension, reasoning and emotional stability. Interestingly, all 16 qualities reflect to some extent Hippocrates' four types. Although the number of precise possibilities kept changing, researchers appeared to agree about the basic qualities.

In the 1960s, the German-born psychologist Hans Eysenck decided to reduce the list dramatically, to only three dimensions: extroversion/introversion (sociable vs. reserved); neurotic/stable (moody and anxious vs. calm); and psychoticism (aggressive and hostile vs. less confrontational and suspicious). Like Hippocrates, Eysenck believed that personality has a biological basis, and that it is enduring and stable. He also promoted the idea that each personality characteristic is best imagined as lying on a spectrum, a continuous dimension between two extremes. He believed that most of us will fall somewhere within the extremes on each of the dimensions.

The idea that personality is stable – that when circumstances change, it's unlikely to make much difference to the way we express ourselves – was assumed throughout all the arguments about how many traits need to be considered. However, this belief (never proven, by the way) was first seriously challenged in the late 1960s by Professor Walter Mischel at Stanford University in California. Mischel believed that the way we behave, particularly when we're children, depends heavily on the circumstances in which we find ourselves at the time we're being observed. He devised a 'temptation' test, to see how stable the quality of one trait, impulsivity, might be. This test, now quite famous, has come to be known as the 'Marshmallow Test'.

Mischel gave young children a choice: either they could have a small treat – a marshmallow, cookie or pretzel – straight away; or, if they waited for about 15 minutes, they could have two of these treats. Children differed dramatically. Some were unable to resist the tempting treat, while others were able to hold out for a double reward. His research did indeed illustrate how temptation, one of many possible environmental circumstances, can influence and change our behaviour. Interestingly, follow-up studies on these children many years later showed how stable the impulsivity dimension actually is, and how dependably it links with some other personality characteristics. Perhaps the lesson here is that some traits are indeed fairly stable when we look at the long term, but when we're young, our behaviour is less predictable, more determined by the circumstances in each situation than by our inherent qualities.

For many years, the 'state–trait debate' – whether personality can be described as stable and enduring, or whether there's no point talking about traits because our behaviour depends on the situation we're in – raged among psychologists. As so often happens when an academic argument becomes polarised like this – when advocates line up on either side of a debate consisting of totally opposite viewpoints – the argument gradually settles down and most people are content to accept a middle ground. Nowadays, psychologists try to tease out the extent to which traits are stable, rather than simply to argue that they are either inherited and stable, or learned and volatile.

Most psychologists in the field of personality today work from a list of five major personality dimensions. These were constructed after careful and extensive statistical research. They're known as 'the Big Five', and the names most commonly linked to their development are the psychologists Robert McRae and Paul Costa. The Big Five are listed below with a description of the sort of behaviour you would expect of individuals scoring at the extreme ends of each dimension. These five traits are considered the most heavily genetically loaded and therefore the most stable expressions of our personality. I've included some recent estimates of the extent to which each is thought to be inherited – that is, how stable and enduring each is considered to be. These are listed below, from least to most consistent. After each term, you will see the words I will be using to refer to either end of each of these five dimensions:

1. *Agreeableness* (41–42% inherited): compassionate, affectionate, cooperative, good-natured, helpful *vs.* suspicious, unsympathetic, critical, rude. Our terms: good-natured *vs.* unsympathetic.
2. *Neuroticism* (41–48%): tense, moody, hostile, vulnerable, unhappy *vs.* calm, even-tempered, secure. Our terms: moody *vs.* calm.
3. *Conscientiousness* (44–49%): hard-working, dependable, competent, organised *vs.* impulsive, careless, disorganised. Our terms: organised *vs.* careless.
4. *Extraversion* (53–54%): sociable, energetic, stimulation-seeking, outgoing *vs.* quiet, reserved, withdrawn. Our terms: outgoing *vs.* reserved.
5. *Openness to experience* (57–61%): curious, adventurous, independent, imaginative *vs.* practical, conventional, liking of routine. Our terms: adventurous *vs.* predictable.

As you can see, there's no agreement yet about the extent of the heritability of each of these five characteristics. Nonetheless, most researchers do agree that these five dimensions represent the most powerful and enduring aspects of human personality. They are therefore the ones you'll want to focus on, the ones that will help most when you work out which of your children are most likely to get along well easily, and which are likely to clash no matter how hard you try to maintain peace at home! These five traits are the ones you'll want to work *with*, rather than try to change, in your children.

Parents generally read the descriptions of the five dimensions and know immediately which side of each dimension best describes their child. These are, however, dimensions – continua – as opposed to black and white categories, so some children may seem neither one nor the other with regard to one or more of the traits. If you're unsure where your child falls along any of these dimensions, there are a number of good quizzes online that you can use to help you.

The Big Five personality traits: who gets along best with whom?

In a moment we'll discuss the effects of the Big Five personality dimensions. First, however, it's important to point out that there are many other personality traits, for example bravery, charm, frankness or wittiness, that appear to be much more malleable – in other words, they depend heavily on specific circumstances and on how we learn to behave. As a consequence, you should be able to teach your children how to manage these characteristics, how to behave differently if they're constantly arguing. This is best achieved by behaving yourself as you hope your children will behave, and to offer specific suggestions – ways of behaving differently that you explain clearly – and praise when your children make the effort to modify their habitual response. You'll learn more in Part 2 about how to solve disputes and arguments that may arise when personalities clash.

When it comes to the Big Five, however, it's best not to insist that your children try to change their behaviour dramatically. Instead, it will be much easier for everyone if you learn to recognise the extent to which each of your children exhibits these traits, and use that information as a sort of 'advance warning system', as information that will help you know which interactions to encourage and which to avoid when possible.

As far as I am aware, there is no published research that can tell us which personality dimensions are associated with the most compatible and incompatible personality types among children. There are, however, a number of studies that focus on adult personality characteristics and attempt to use them to predict compatibility between colleagues, friends and partners. We cannot, of course, map these results for adults directly onto children or onto sibling relationships. This is because children are still developing their social skills and, more important, because each type of relationship – siblings, partners, friends, colleagues – has different rules governing the interactions that take place within them. Nonetheless, the results of these studies can give us some clues that will help predict best compatibility among siblings.

Personality studies on adults

In the workplace, Susan Kichuk and Willi Weisner at the US International University in California found that the most successful business teams are those in which all members are highly extrovert and agreeable, while scoring low on neuroticism. Studies on couple relationships, and there are many, tend almost invariably to find that couples in which one or both score high on neuroticism are less likely to feel satisfied with their relationship. This isn't, of course, surprising, either in relationships or, for that matter, in most other circumstances!

Looking at the other extreme, the dimension most strongly associated with relationship satisfaction is agreeableness – again, no surprise. A little more intriguing, however, is the finding that openness to experience, extroversion and conscientiousness have all been linked to more satisfying and enduring couple relationships. This finding goes against the perceived wisdom that 'opposites attract'. One study of couples, carried out by Krista Gattis and her colleagues in California, looked specifically at whether 'likes' or 'opposites' make the best match. They found that there was no significant association between similarity of partner personalities and marital satisfaction. In other words, there appears to be no need for individuals to be alike on the dimensions of agreeableness or conscientiousness, not at least for them to feel happy in their relationship.

These studies provide us with a great starting point. The findings can help you predict which of your children is likely to get along best in terms of their respective personalities, and which relationships may need a bit more supervision and guidance so those siblings can bond well despite a possible clash of personality.

Let's turn now to specifics. How can our current knowledge about personality help you understand better the potential for bonding between your children and feel better equipped for the flashpoints? In the discussion that follows, I've drawn on some research, but because there is such a limited amount of it (and none I could find that deals with children's relationships with their siblings), I will rely far more on clinical experience.

Your behaviour as your children's role model matters most

Nothing is as likely to influence your children's ways of behaving and interacting as much as the way you yourself behave. You are, and always will be, their most important role model. Therefore, the way you interact with others matters – even when you don't think they're observing you. If you take care to show kindness, generosity, fairness and an even-handed approach when interacting with other people, if you think through calmly and logically how to react when under stress rather than simply lashing out angrily, and if you show a genuine interest in what's going on and a lively appetite for new learning and fresh experiences, your children are more likely to grow up to be sociable, likeable, fair-minded individuals who believe they can rise to any challenge life might throw at them. They're also more likely to grow up liking and respecting one another.

Sibling compatibility with regard to the Big Five personality traits

Openness to experience (adventurous vs. practical)

If one of your children is adventurous while the other is more practical and conventional, they're quite likely to get on – that is, as long as you've taught them the importance of compromise and mutual respect. In these pairings, the outgoing, adventurous sibling will bring the other one out, while the more reserved and practical child will encourage less risk-taking behaviour in their sibling.

This assumes, however, that the age gap – and therefore the levels of understanding and physical ability – of the pair are relatively similar. If the age gap is great (more than four years) and the older child is incredibly adventurous, then there's the worry that the older one will encourage adventures that could frighten, even endanger, a reserved or timid younger child. If you sense that this might be happening, it will be important to keep a close eye on them. Make sure, too, to praise your older child whenever they help or protect the younger one, rather than when they expose them to risk. So for example, if the older one emphasises the importance of wearing a helmet when riding a bicycle and they wear a helmet themselves, well and good. If, on the other hand, they dare the younger one to try riding a bicycle without stabilisers before they're ready, you need to intervene.

Remember that if you want to see some real change, always suggest a specific more acceptable approach rather than merely condemning the risky behaviour that caused you to step in.

Extroversion (outgoing vs. reserved)

If your children are all outgoing, there's no reason to worry that they won't get on, although you may need to keep an eye on their collective wanderlust! At the other extreme, if your children are all fairly reserved, their relationship is unlikely to be as close as those whose adventurous spirits have meant they've shared numerous challenging experiences.

Even so, reserved children are often quite compatible, accepting and understanding of the 'space' each of them needs.

If one child is very outgoing and the other reserved, you may have to remind your more outgoing child to respect their sibling's need for calm and quiet, and encourage them to satisfy their outgoing tendencies by seeking out like-minded friends.

Conscientiousness (organised vs. careless)

If all your children are quite neat and organised, or, at the other extreme, if they all tend to be rather careless and disorganised, they'll be less likely to quarrel about living conditions if they share a bedroom. If, however, you put a very conscientious child into a bedroom with one who's untidy and more disorganised, hoping the tidy one will 'reform' the other, you're asking for trouble! All this does is ensure that you'll be spending a great deal of time refereeing disputes. If such a situation is inevitable because of space limitations in your home, it would be a good idea to create a division in the room, and encourage each child to keep their own area in order according to the standards that you establish, standards that represent an acceptable compromise to each of them.

The finding that couples rate their relationships as more satisfying if either, but particularly, the male is more conscientious suggests that conscientiousness is a desirable trait to many people – certainly to adult females. This finding suggests that a conscientious, dependable child is quite likely to be regarded favourably by their peers – as long as they don't hold rigid standards. Therefore, such behaviour is to be encouraged.

Neuroticism (moody vs. calm)

Children who are very unalike on this dimension are more liable to get on well than those who are similarly moody and anxious. The presence of a calm, even-tempered child will soothe their anxious sibling, and a caring/cared-for bond is likely to develop. A child who is very moody will also get on well with a highly agreeable child, and they'll feel comforted in their presence.

Moody children may well try to avoid siblings who are highly outgoing or adventurous, although they may look up to (or, on the less positive side, they might envy) their siblings' devil-may-care attitude. A moody child might also feel soothed by the predictability offered by a sibling who's very organised. On the other hand, they may feel anxious and threatened by a careless, disorganised sibling. A more even-tempered child, however, is likely to get on well with most people, particularly those who are reserved and/or practical.

Agreeableness (good-natured vs. unsympathetic)

Highly agreeable children are a gift to any parent. They'll get on with any and all siblings, and their sunny presence will soothe anxious children in particular. Unsympathetic children – those who are not so agreeable – will also get on best with their polar opposite. In fact, this is one case where opposites do indeed make an excellent pairing. A highly agreeable child who's also moderately adventurous can help to bring out the best in a sibling who's unsympathetic, and a caring/cared-for relationship is likely to develop.

Summary

Your child's personality will develop and change as they mature, although the five traits we've discussed in this chapter will remain fairly stable compared to other characteristics. It's therefore helpful to become aware of the way your children behave with regard to the 'Big Five', because you cannot expect major changes on these dimensions – at least, it won't be easy for them to change.

The child who will need the most input from you is a moody child. Now that you know how deeply this is embedded in their nature, I hope that rather than criticising them, you'll try to help them change their outlook and become more calm and trusting. It will help if they spend time with highly agreeable children in particular, and those children will naturally wish to help calm an anxious sibling. Those who are more organised and/or practically minded can also be excellent role models for a moody child.

Often, children who can be described as being at opposite ends of a dimension will still manage to get on well, although they may not feel as close to one another as those who are similar in character. This will be the case with regard to four of the five major personality dimensions. The exception is the dimension of conscientiousness.

Finally, if your child is highly agreeable by nature, they'll not only get along with just about everyone, but they're also likely to bring out the best in others. However, even children who don't find it easy to be good-natured and to think the best of others can learn to behave more agreeably. You'll want to encourage this particular quality above all others if you want to give your children the best chance of getting on well with one another, and with other people generally. Set a good example yourself, and offer specific tactics whenever you see a good opportunity to do so.

There's always the possibility of compatibility, even though at times you may feel like despairing. Remember, experience works on all of us, even those who show the most extreme personality characteristics. It will be well worthwhile, therefore, for you to look out for, praise and encourage any behaviours you feel will help your children get on well, particularly any cooperative, thoughtful and affectionate behaviour you notice. This will help everyone get on better, as well as to feel happier and more secure.

Of course, temperament is only one piece of the puzzle that can help you understand your children's relationships better and allows them to develop the most positive bonds possible, along with age and gender differences and number of children in the family.

There are two further factors that influence the quality and depth of the sibling relationships. These are your child's birth order position, and your own experiences when you were growing up.

4

Birth order

Adopting three children taught me a great deal about the powerful effect that birth order position has on our behaviour and attitudes. Technically, each of my three is a firstborn. However, over the years each has taken on the characteristics associated with their position in our family – eldest, middle and youngest. This transformation made it clear to me that the characteristics typically associated with each birth order position are learned, and that they contribute generously to the formation of our character.

In this chapter, you'll learn about the characteristics that are most typical of each birth order position, and how those qualities shape certain aspects of our character; in particular, how we interact when we're with others, especially in small groups. Your knowledge of these effects will in turn help you understand more clearly how and why your children behave towards one another in the ways they do. I also offer some suggestions about how you can give each of them the best chance to build positive, lasting bonds with their siblings.

Why birth order effects are so powerful

The human brain develops most rapidly between about three weeks after conception, when the brain, spinal cord and major organs begin to form, and about five years of age. Although our brain is not fully organised until we're well into our teenage years, the most spectacular and dramatic neurological development occurs during the first five years of life. The experiences we have during this period help to establish brain 'wiring' – that is, they're instrumental in laying down the basic framework that determines how we think, feel and behave throughout the rest of our lives.

Of course, because psychological growth is the result of a complex interaction between our unique genetic make-up and our ongoing experience, and because we never stop learning, we continue to change and develop throughout our lives. However, our early experiences are particularly powerful because they lay down the foundations of character.

Because most sibling pairs are born within four years of one another, the size and shape of a child's family is usually established during their early years, and most of their interactions will centre on parents and siblings during this time. The more often the same behaviours are repeated during those formative years – for example, being encouraged to share toys or to help care for a younger sibling – the more likely it is that these patterns of interacting will become deeply entrenched. As a result, the responses become our 'default' reactions in those and in similar circumstances for the rest of our life. That means that, although we're always capable of learning new ways of responding, our first reaction, particularly when we're tired, or when we're feeling emotional or highly stressed, will continue to be based on the patterns that were established during the first five or six years of life. In the two examples above, we would therefore 'automatically' share what we have and/or help out if someone appeals to us for help.

Typical birth order characteristics

Don't expect that the qualities described below will map perfectly onto each and every eldest, middle and youngest child! Every family is different, and each child develops in response to four main factors: their own genetic make-up, their birth order position, their interactions within their family and friendship groups, and – to a lesser extent – in response to other experiences. Within this framework there will be certain circumstances that are common to children who share the same birth order position. For example, the fact that firstborns are the only children in the family who enjoy exclusive parental attention and then lose it means that they will always try harder than other children to please authority (in other words, parental) figures. Similarly, youngest children, because they have the maximum number of more mature and competent people around to help them when they need it, tend to give up more easily than the others in their family when something they're working on doesn't go to plan. Such circumstances affect character in fairly predictable ways; hence the picture is created of a 'typical' first, middle and youngest.

Here, then, are the most common qualities associated with children in each birth order position. The best way to regard these are as a 'best photo-fit', rather than as a perfect match.

Characteristics of firstborns

The birth of your first child is an overwhelming experience for parents. The event is hugely anticipated, and when the baby arrives, they'll receive relatively more parental care and attention than will any subsequent child. This is partly because everything is so new and exciting, partly because parents have to learn as they go and so proceed more cautiously – often becoming over-attentive – and partly because there are no other children around yet to compete for time and care. As a consequence, firstborns have more opportunities to hear well-formed language and to interact with adults. All this exclusive attention means that they learn to communicate well and to relate skilfully to other people. These abilities will be incredibly valuable throughout their lives, because they are associated with academic success and high EQ, or emotional intelligence.

At the same time, however, because this is a first-time experience for parents, they're likely to be more anxious as they attempt to figure out the best ways to care for their precious baby. By the time the others come along, they'll feel calmer and more experienced. Their heightened anxiety has a knock-on effect, because babies are acutely sensitive to their carers' mood state and are likely to match the moods they sense. As a result, the eldest child tends to be more anxious than their younger siblings.

Firstborns also tend to set very high expectations for themselves. We set our standards in relation to the people we're around most often, and firstborns spend most of their time early on with adults, who of course appear to a little child to be totally capable and competent beings. Therefore, in matching this, these children ask a great deal of themselves. Throughout their life, they set the bar high and push themselves hard. A desirable consequence is that they're more likely to end up in positions of leadership; but at the same time, because they push themselves so hard, they're more prone than others to overwork and burnout.

When a new sibling comes along, the adjustment is much greater for firstborns than it will be for any other subsequent child. They, and they alone, have to learn to share the parental care and attention they'd previously enjoyed without competition. That loss of exclusivity leaves many firstborns with an unquenchable desire for approval throughout their lives, particularly from those who are in positions of power and authority – from representative parental figures, as it were.

They're also more likely than their younger siblings to be well organised, responsible, nurturing and caring. They repeat these behaviours because they discover early on that if they help look after the 'new competition' rather than sulk because they're no longer centre stage, they regain some of the parental attention they crave.

Firstborns' relationships with their siblings

Firstborns love to act as teachers and carers. Given half a chance, they'll take complete charge of their younger siblings, issuing instructions and making decisions about who does what. This gives them back a sense of control and, if done in accordance with parental guidance, is likely to earn them praise for helping to manage and look after the little ones.

Sometimes, however, a firstborn will take things too far and try to take over the parental role entirely with regard to the younger ones – usually more so than the often rebellious younger child wants or will tolerate. They do this for any of a number of reasons. Taking charge may help them feel more in control again of what's happening to them. If the younger sibling doesn't want the controls imposed on them, the older child may persist in bossing the little ones around as a sort of 'disguised aggression', a way of showing their jealousy while at the same time appearing to be 'helpful'. Or they may take over too completely as a compensatory behaviour: when we miss someone or the attention they once gave us, one way of coping with the loss is to step into their role, to act as if we 'are' the person we're missing.

The relationships firstborns forge with their siblings tend to be strong but unequal, with the younger ones looking up to their big brother or sister for support and guidance and the firstborn helping but sometimes controlling too much. The most balanced relationships in terms of power are usually between a brother and a sister, because their gender difference allows them to stop competing quite so hard to appear special and unique in their parents' eyes – after all, each is already easily distinguishable from the other.

Finally, although I wish it were not so, there still tends to be a gender difference in terms of the way firstborns relate to their sisters and brothers, at least in the early years. Girls more often use words to direct and instruct, whereas boys rely more on action to convey their messages.

What parents can do to encourage good relationships between firstborns and their siblings

Inadvertently, parents often contribute to the over-controlling, bossy behaviours that make younger children want to distance themselves from their big brother or sister, by rewarding helping behaviour exclusively. The key to helping create a good relationship between firstborns and their siblings is balance.

Do encourage and praise helping behaviours. This not only lightens the burden for you, but it also allows firstborns to learn how to care for and nurture those who are less capable than they are. This is a skill that will give them many opportunities for leadership, and stand them in good stead throughout their lives. Equally often, however, remember to praise them for other sorts of positive behaviour; for practising the piano or bringing home a lovely drawing they made at school, for example. Be sure, too, to spend some one-to-one time with your firstborn on a regular basis. The amount of time you spend together is far less important than the quality of that time. The best thing you can do is something they enjoyed with you before the new baby came along. For example, you could read them a bedtime story each evening, even if it means an earlier bedtime for the younger child. That way, the older child will still feel special and cared for, and therefore not feel compelled to work through the baby to gain your attention. They'll also become less anxious and more self-confident generally – a win for everyone.

Characteristics of middle children

We tend to think of middle children as the 'black sheep' of the family; outsiders, troubled and unhappy people. In truth, this isn't the case at all. Middle children are often the most socially skilled individuals in the family, good at negotiation and compromise. Statistically, they're also the child who is least likely to seek psychological help when they're older.

Middle children are lucky, because they're born to experienced parents who have already learned a great deal about how to parent from their first child. As a result, those parents are more relaxed and confident about what they're doing. Even though they'll probably be more exhausted because of the extra workload they have now with two children to look after, their increased competence and confidence makes for a more relaxed atmosphere at home.

Middles know how to attract attention subtly and skilfully. This is partly because they have to work harder than their older brother or sister had to capture exclusive parental attention (particularly if the two siblings are closely spaced and/or of the same gender, and therefore need parental care for the same things at about the same intervals), and partly because – with demanding siblings on either side of them – the role of peacemaker is often their salvation. Neither a more mature and capable older child, nor the cute little attention-getting baby, middles need to find a special way to gain their share of care and attention, too.

Whereas firstborns identify with their parents most readily, middle-borns are more attuned to their peers and are likely to identify most strongly with them. Because they grow up surrounded by other children, their natural tendency is to base their goals and standards on individuals who are roughly their own age.

Herein lies a vulnerability for middle-borns, particularly during adolescence, and particularly for those who tend by nature to be impulsive. If middle children align themselves with the 'wrong' peer group, they're more likely than a law-abiding firstborn to follow the crowd one step too far and find themselves in trouble. Middles find it very difficult to show opposition to group decisions and to take the risk of being rejected by their friends. This is hard enough for any child, but harder still for one whose identity is strongly determined by their peers.

At the same time, middle-borns profit from a positive aspect of peer-based identity. Whereas firstborns often set overly ambitious, highly challenging targets for themselves (based as these are on adult role models), middle-borns are fairly realistic about what they can achieve. They also tend to be less fiercely competitive than their older brother or sister, and they're less likely to pit themselves against their peers. This makes them more sociable, good companions who are a welcome addition to almost any group.

Finally, middle-borns are more likely than other children in the family to take up 'causes', to work for organisations that support the underprivileged or downtrodden. They're also the most likely child in the family to go through a phase of looking outlandish – dressing unusually, sporting extreme hairstyles or wearing eccentric make-up, particularly in early adolescence. Both of these tendencies – supporting those who've been overlooked and drawing attention to their appearance – are probably the middle child's way of reacting when they feel overlooked or left out in the bustle of family life. Their eccentricities, while serving to offload some of the resentment these children probably feel, have the added advantage of making middle children appear more interesting and attractive to those around them.

Middle children's relationships with their siblings

Middle-borns make great companions. They usually have well-developed social skills, although sometimes their strong need to fit in with those around them means that the others will take advantage of this ability and encourage them to test out house rules and boundaries.

They're generally calm and equable, and as a result they're almost always included as a welcome addition to their peer group. They don't demand that others pay attention to them, nor do they insist that things are done their way – these characteristics are more often seen in last-borns and firstborns respectively. They're regarded as interesting, sometimes even 'quirky', and others are drawn to them.

If you have a middle child or children in your family, you're lucky. You have a good social leveller.

What you can do to encourage good relationships between middle-borns and their siblings

Without being particularly aware that they're doing so, middle-borns respond to environmental demands by doing what fits in best with the prevailing mood. As a consequence, and without you having to do anything at all, they'll probably get on well with their siblings.

However, look out. After a while, responding first to everyone else can sometimes erode their own sense of direction, their own concept of who they are as an individual, a person apart from their peers and siblings. To encourage high self-esteem, you can really help by spending some regular one-on-one time with your middle-born. On these occasions, encourage them to talk about what they want for themselves, about their own hopes and dreams. You could, for example, take your middle child out for a pizza once a fortnight, or take them shopping and encourage them to choose clothing or whatever they need on their own, without regard for the others in the family.

If your children are all the same gender, or if the firstborn is a different gender from the second-born, relationships will probably be maintained with less friction than if the first two are of one gender and the third of another. This is more because of the firstborn's need for parental attention than any quality inherent in the middle child; nevertheless, it's often the middle child who can feel most stressed in these circumstances. The firstborn is likely to be jealous of the little one, who's not only regarded by parents as cute and special, the baby of the group, but also because at the same time, parents regard the new arrival as another (special) firstborn because they're the first of that gender in the family.

The firstborn's reaction to this apparent affront is to redirect their perceived loss of control towards the middle child. Well aware of how easy it can be to sway their sibling, they may even encourage the biddable middle to 'side' with them and reject or tease the new arrival. If you suspect that this is happening, by all means encourage the strengthened bond between the first two, but at the same time praise the two older ones for behaving positively towards the new arrival whenever there's even the slightest opportunity to do so.

Difficult as it will seem with so many children to look after now, you're most likely to achieve harmony among them in the same ways you did when you only had two to look after – by finding ways to spend some enjoyable time one to one with each child, and by praising behaviours and qualities in each of them that emphasises their uniqueness and their kindness towards one another. That way, all of them will grow up with a better sense of self, and in particular the middle child will feel freer to develop close bonds with their siblings.

Characteristics of last-born children

Many of us who are not last-borns feel envious of those who are. Last-born children appear to be indulged, even spoiled, and to be allowed to get away with things that would never have been tolerated from the older children in the family. Any mistakes or inadequacies seem to be excused. They seem to get away with being less tidy and more disorganised than their older brothers and sisters. And whenever last-borns ask for help – and quite often they do – someone usually hurries to their rescue.

However, being a last-born isn't always as enviable as appearance suggests. Without realising it, parents of the baby in the family often give the little one mixed messages about the costs and benefits of growing up and becoming independent.

On the one hand, parents are glad to leave the sleepless nights and constant caring that young children demand behind them. At the same time, however, they often start to feel wistful about their last 'baby' becoming independent and leaving home. This leaves last-borns unsure whether to strive for independence, or to remain dependent and 'cute', and appeal for help whenever anything challenges them.

Last-borns also often suffer from low self-esteem. Like firstborns, although less dramatically so, they're surrounded by role models who are all more mature, and therefore more competent, than they are. Their usual reaction is to set themselves high and often unrealistic standards.

In addition, last-borns are rarely allowed to struggle to complete tasks by themselves because another member of the family is usually on hand to step in and help, eager to feel useful and to prove their worth. As a result, last-borns rarely know the pride that comes with working hard to achieve something difficult.

Last-borns are often considered to be highly creative. This doesn't come about by chance. Just like the others before them, they have a strong need to distinguish themselves from their siblings. However, they'll probably only be able to do so if they develop an unusual talent or interest, because their older siblings have no doubt already distinguished themselves in more mainstream ways; for example ,through academic or sporting achievement. Therefore, their only options are generally in the more creative domains – drama, music, acting and artistic expression.

In one sense, they're lucky. Had the firstborn chosen to pursue drama or painting, for example, or any activity other than academic prowess, the quality that parents usually value most highly, their parent would probably have steered them back to those highly valued pursuits, perhaps stifling a true talent. Last-borns, if they are artistic, have a better chance of developing their gift.

Last-borns very often appear to be daring, willing to take big risks. Unlike middle children, this isn't because they want to fit in and please others. This is instead the result of a set of much more complex circumstances. First, parents tend to indulge the 'baby' in the family. They'll allow the little one to get away with breaking the rules more often than they would ever have allowed their older children. Second, by the time the third or fourth child comes along, parents are busier and therefore less likely to take the time to notice when their house rules are being infringed.

Furthermore, parents are also more experienced by the time the last one comes along, and as a result, they've come to realise that many of their 'golden rules' were unnecessarily strict. It's in the nature of all children to push against and test the limits that parents set for them, and of course last-borns are no exception. So what happens? The youngest child has much wider boundaries to challenge than did their older brothers and sisters. Thus they have to take greater risks to challenge the disciplinary boundaries.

Last-borns' relationships with their siblings

Most older siblings want to help look after the younger children. This is great – to a degree. As you know, however, it's all too easy for older siblings to take over completely, to direct and control the little ones more than those (more risk-taking) younger children can easily tolerate.

When a sibling relationship is based entirely on helping/being helped, the relationship is likely to become tense and fraught, with lots of arguments and defiant behaviour. On the other hand, if the younger child is utterly compliant, they'll allow the older child to take over completely. As a result, they may not discover or express their own unique abilities until much later in life, when they're living independently.

Older siblings are often drawn to the little one because of their apparent creative flair and their tendency to defy authority more often than the older one would ever dare. The little one will in turn look up to their older siblings, copying their behaviour and following them around eagerly, because they appear to them to be so competent and so capable.

Once they reach adolescence, however, the younger sibling will start to feel the stronger pull of their peer group. At that point they're likely to find the 'I'm in charge' approach of their older sibling stifling, even patronising. At the same time, because they too want to spend more time with their peers, the older sibling may start to feel burdened by the need to care for a needy little brother or sister! They may become distant and, without parental encouragement, this may become habitual.

For these reasons, in order to encourage this particular relationship – that of eldest and youngest – parents are well advised to enforce regular family occasions such as mealtimes and any holiday traditions they established early on.

> ## FLASHPOINT
>
> *My older children accuse me of 'babying' my youngest and perhaps it's true. Is this bad for my children's relationships with each other?*
>
> I'm afraid it's not only detrimental to the sibling relationships; if you are babying your youngest, you're not doing them any favours either. Every child hopes to be the apple of their parents' eye, and they think they'll enjoy all that lavish care and attention. In truth, treating a child as if they're dependent and unable to take care of themselves is associated with lower self-esteem. Children may say they don't want to have to take responsibility for themselves, but the more they do so, the greater their sense of self-worth and self-pride will be.
>
> If you treat each child as if you expect them to become competent, they're more likely to try to prove your expectations. Furthermore, when you're treating them all equally in this regard, they're less likely to feel jealousy or a sense of unfairness. You may even increase the chances that they'll want to start helping each other!

What you can do to encourage good relationships between last-borns and their siblings

Last-borns who see themselves as independent and capable are most likely to develop great relationships with their siblings. When they know that they can do things for themselves when necessary, they're more likely to enjoy the help that's offered without feeling overprotected or overly confined.

Parents can help their last-borns grow up feeling self-confident if they make a point of encouraging that child, whenever possible, to tackle new challenges themselves. There should be little, if any, stepping in to help the 'baby'.

Second, parents must be careful not to reward older siblings excessively when they 'do for' the little one. It's much better to encourage activities that involve more equality, activities that demand teamwork to overcome problems and meet challenges, than it is always to praise helping behaviours. For example, parents might ask the children to erect a tent so they can camp in the garden, or plan and prepare a meal together. It's also good practice to praise the older sibling for encouraging the younger ones to achieve somethings independently. The key is for the entire family to empower their youngest member, rather than stepping in and doing for them.

On the whole, everyone enjoys spending time with the baby of the family, so – unless the older child is in the company of friends to whom they wish to 'show off' – the last-born will usually be welcomed to join in whatever is happening at the time.

In summary, as long as parents encourage independence in their youngest and teamwork among all their children, their last-born is highly likely to develop strong and positive relationships with their older siblings.

Summary of factors that affect 'typical' birth order characteristics

Age gap

- If there's a small age gap between siblings – two years or less – the typical birth order characteristics will probably describe children in each birth order position fairly accurately.
- If, however, there is a wider gap – four years or more – things become more complicated. The relatively late arrival of the next child means that the older one has had time to settle into patterns of behaviour typical of a last-born, because during the greater part of their early years they were treated as the youngest in the family.
- When the age gap is small, siblings will have similar needs at similar times. As a result, they're likely to think of their sibling as a rival more than as a companion, especially early on when both children are clamouring for parental attention. However, as you know, these intense feelings aren't all bad. They mean that later on, those two children are likely to enjoy a close relationship. Therefore, never despair if a sibling relationship is often fiery when the children are young. That intensity will help them bond as they age.
- When the age gap between two siblings is large, a caring/cared-for relationship is the most likely outcome. To ensure closeness, a more balanced relationship as well as the minimum resentment when

they're older, parents would be wise to encourage the two of them to cooperate as equals, at least some of the time.

Gender

- In families where all the children are the same gender, their birth order characteristics are likely to describe them fairly accurately. However, if one child is different – say you have three children, one girl and two boys – that one child will have some characteristics of a firstborn, whatever position they occupy in the pecking order, in addition to possessing qualities typical for their birth order position relative to the other two. This is because parents treat the child of the different gender as a 'first' daughter or son.
- Siblings of the same gender are likely to be close. At the same time, however, they'll be more competitive than boy–girl pairs, because there's less to distinguish one from the other. This will be particularly noticeable when the age gap between them is small.

Family size

- The more children there are in a family, the more socially skilled, adaptable and cooperative they're likely to be. Children in large families – more than three – tend to get on fairly well because they're used to sharing and to welcoming new family members. They get plenty of practice accepting compromise, so they're unlikely to expect always to have things their own way.
- The relationships between siblings will vary in strength and intimacy, although the closest relationships are usually between the eldest child and younger children (a caring/cared-for bond), and between pairs who are close in age (a powerful mix of rivalry and companionship).
- It's interesting to observe that when there are lots of children – more than four – the children will frequently break into smaller friendship groups. Pairs of children (or sometimes three of them), usually those who are closest in age, form particularly close bonds. Within each sub-group, the older child will generally take on the characteristics of a firstborn or leader, while the others enjoy a more submissive 'follower' role. When the children grow up, these sub-groups tend to reassemble whenever the family gets together.

A note on multiple births

- People often assume that twins (or triplets) will define themselves in terms of who is the firstborn and who is the baby – and go on to develop the relevant characteristics. In fact, this rarely happens. Instead, a twin's main concern, just as it is for every other child, is to distinguish themselves so that they appear special to their parents. That means that they're more likely to compete fiercely with one another for unique status than to concern themselves with first- and last-born roles (unless, of course, each feels that gives them distinctive and important status in their parents' eyes).
- However, because twins share so many experiences, they'll also be close. The result is complicated – an incredibly strong bond that's laced with ambivalence.
- The nature of a twin relationship is discussed in more detail in Part 4, Chapter 16.
- Twins' relationships with their other siblings will almost certainly be less intense than their bond with one another – and unfortunately it will also be less positive. The problem for the others is the 'novelty value' of multiple-birth babies. Twins are more common nowadays in the West, largely because there was a practice of implanting several eggs in each cycle during early fertility treatments. Nevertheless, despite the increase, twins and triplets are still rare enough to fascinate. Because of the positive attention they attract, their other siblings are likely to feel left out, neither special nor interesting, and this can cause envy and jealousy.
- If you have twins, you must therefore be especially vigilant about how you distribute your attention, and you would be well advised to remind visitors to respond as 'equally' as possible to each child. Siblings of twins will only develop supportive relationships if each child feels important and special, and no one feels left out.

A note on step-siblings and birth order

You might think that if step-siblings are introduced into a family, each child will assume a 'new' birth order position, and go on to develop the characteristics of that new position. In fact, this rarely happens. Turn to page 187 for more about what happens to sibling relationships when step-siblings are introduced into the family.

Summary

Age gaps, gender differences and temperament all help to determine which children in the family are likely to get on best with which others. The birth order position of each also matters, but more in relation to the quality of relationships than their intensity.

A firstborn/last-born or firstborn/middle-child bond is likely to take the form of caring/cared-for, although if the age difference between them is small and parents encourage them to cooperate whenever possible, the relationship will be less skewed. These are generally the strongest, most long-lasting sibling relationships. Firstborns are attracted to the 'wilder', more risk-taking behaviour of last-borns – behaviours they would love to acquire but dare not do so – and to the co-operative nature of the more easy-going middle child. At the same time, both middle children and last-borns will look to the eldest for organisation, guidance and leadership.

Relationships between middle children and last-borns – and in larger families, middles with other middles – will generally be amiable, although not necessarily close, unless they're extremely close in age and/or of the same gender. In that case, rivalry and competitiveness will be the predominant feature early on; closeness the defining quality later.

Together, these factors – age gap, gender, temperament and birth order characteristics – are the main ingredients that determine the quality and intensity of sibling relationships. However, we're still missing one vital ingredient: parents' attitudes to and beliefs about parenting. Their approach will be highly influenced by the way they themselves were parented and by the relationships they formed with their own siblings when they were children.

It's time, therefore, to take a look at the development of parental attitudes to parenting, and the effect those attitudes have on their children's relationships with each other.

5

Your own childhood experience and relationships

The relationships between your children will be shaped by a number of factors, but there is one that stands out; one that has far more impact than any other. That one factor is how you parent your children. The ways you look after each child, how you help them sort out problems and resolve differences with others, and – most critically – how you conduct your own life, will create the blueprint for their own approach to life's challenges. Your behaviour and attitudes will also shape the ways they interact with others, now and for the rest of their lives.

What a daunting task! And where do parents go to learn how to do this, the most important job you'll probably ever do?

Few of us get the chance to learn about different ways we might parent. As soon as your first baby arrives, you're simply expected to know what to do. The only experience most of us have to draw on is the way we ourselves were parented, and what we learned from the other people in our family when we were growing up.

Between 1989 and 1992, Glen Elder, Rand Conger and their colleagues at the University of Iowa carried out a longitudinal study to look at, among a number of other factors, the effects that different parenting styles have on children's attitudes and outlook on life. Their subjects were 451 two-parent families living in rural Iowa. In each family there was one 13-year-old child (the 'target' child) and one other child within four years of age of the target child. During the four years of the study, the researchers visited the families in their homes on numerous occasions. They interviewed all the family members, asked them to fill out questionnaires, and videotaped sibling and parent interactions on a number of occasions. The researchers also set them a number of challenges as a family and videotaped them as they attempted to solve the problems. They collected a great deal of other data as well; in particular, information about the parents' own family of origin, and their attitudes to parenting.

Many valuable observations came out of this study, but the ones that concern us most in this chapter are the factors that influenced parenting practices. Time and again, both mothers and fathers told the researchers that they believed the way they were parented as children was one of the strongest influences shaping their own parenting attitudes and style. This was backed up by the videotapes, particularly when it came to the reproduction of strict parenting methods, but also – to a lesser extent – with regard to a supportive parenting approach.

Of course, parenting style isn't the only influence during your childhood that determines how you now care for your own children. The way your parents treated you in relation to everyone else in your family, as well as the experiences you shared both with your siblings and with your family as a whole, worked together with parenting style to make a deep impact on you during your formative years. Observations of family interactions during the Iowa study backed up what the parents said during the interviews; that when we become parents, we're most likely to reproduce the experiences we lived through when we were young.

What, then, are those factors, and how does each of them help shape the relationships between your children?

Parenting style

Nearly two decades before the Iowa Youth and Families Project, Diana Baumrind, a psychologist at the University of California, Berkeley, made a number of visits to the homes of over 100 pre-schoolers and their parents to observe them as they went about their normal family activities. Her aim was to tease out the most important aspects of parenting, to discover the practices that are most closely associated with happy, self-confident children. She isolated four important aspects of parenting and used them to create her model of parenting style. Baumrind's formulation has stood the test of time well; psychologists and educators still use it today.

The four aspects of parenting that Baumrind identified are:

1. Discipline strategies/types of control used
2. Level of warmth and nurturance
3. Styles of communication
4. Parents' expectations of their children.

Using these as her starting pointing, Baumrind created four 'parenting styles'. Her own and subsequent research has been chiefly concerned with the effects that each of these styles has on children's individual development. I will refer to what is known about that, and add – on the basis of clinical evidence, because little if any research has focused on this angle – how each parenting style appears to influence how siblings relate to one another.

Baumrind's four parenting styles

Authoritarian parenting

Authoritarian parents set standards and are consistent about those standards. However, the standards are rigid; parents don't negotiate or involve their children in setting rules as they become more independent. They demand obedience on the basis of an absolute set of rules of conduct. When their children disobey, they're likely to use the withdrawal of approval, even withdrawal of love, to force them to obey. They're often described by their children as 'aloof' or 'cool'. Communication is based more on relaying rules and establishing order than on listening to the child's point of view. These parents rarely see the need to justify their rules or to explain them in detail.

The children of authoritarian parents tend to be proficient, obedient and well-behaved, but at the same time they're often moody and anxious. Their self-esteem tends to be low, they may not feel confident socially, and they prefer to follow rather than to lead.

Authoritarian parents raise children who get on well in terms of respecting house rules and each other's territory. However, their higher than usual anxiety levels, as well as their fear of putting a foot wrong, prevent them from opening up easily to one another, of sharing their vulnerabilities and concerns. As a result, sibling relationships in authoritarian families are not as free and deep as they could be. Later on, they will dutifully stay in contact – they'll remember each other's birthdays and expect to meet up at Christmas and on other traditional family occasions – but the chance that a sibling will become a 'soul mate' is, sadly, remote.

Permissive or 'indulgent' parenting

These parents are accepting and warm towards their children. They spend a great deal of time explaining house rules, and they're likely to involve the children in determining limits and making policy decisions. Even then, they're liable to bend the rules or at least not always to enforce them. They make few demands on their children; for example, in terms of school performance or household responsibility. Permissive parents hope to be considered allies and friends to their children, and for their children to see them as a resource but not to feel the need to live up to any standards they may set for themselves.

The children of permissive parents tend to be impulsive and to be regarded by others as immature. They're rebellious or defiant when their wishes are challenged, and, as a result, they may experience problems with authority figures at school, and later on at work. They tend to give up easily if a task is challenging, and they avoid taking positions of responsibility. As a result, they often perform poorly at school and have difficulty reaching senior positions at work.

There are a great number of arguments and squabbles over territory and pecking order in homes where parents are permissive and indulgent. Because interactions are so often highly emotional and no parent comes in to establish the rules, siblings develop ambivalent feelings towards one another. On the one hand they're rivalrous, but at the same time they feel quite close to one another because of the intensity of their interactions. Later on, they usually remain close, although whenever they get together the old unresolved issues, such as who's in charge of what and what belongs to whom, are likely to resurface, although with a more light-hearted than a bitter taste, making get-togethers lively, but not consistently satisfying.

Uninvolved parenting

Like permissive parents, uninvolved parents make few demands on their children and seldom set limits. Unlike permissive parents, however, their attitude towards their children could not be described as warm or accepting, and they spend little time talking or listening to them. Instead, their attitude is more like that of authoritarian parents – aloof and cool. At the extreme, uninvolved parents may neglect, or even reject, their children.

These children, like those of permissive parents, have difficulties with impulse control. They suffer from low self-esteem and low mood. They frequently perform poorly at school, and they see themselves as less competent than their peers. Rates of delinquency are likely to be high and levels of achievement in school, and later on in work, are usually low, far lower than their actual capabilities.

Siblings of uninvolved parents are rarely close, although they may often argue over resources or territory. Their lack of intimacy is partly because there are few, if any, communal family activities to bring them together, and partly because their impulsive nature and low self-esteem makes it difficult for them to feel close to anyone.

Authoritative parenting

Authoritative parents place great importance on their role as parents. They set high standards for all their children, while at the same time doing their best to treat each child as a unique individual who is worthy of respect. They're warm and nurturing, but although they praise their child's present abilities, they encourage them to strive to be even better in future. Authoritative parents encourage their children to share their views and opinions with the rest of the family, and to make their own decisions and learn from their mistakes. At the same time, they offer clear rules and boundaries so their children know where they stand and when they've done well.

Children of authoritative parents were regarded by Baumrind as the best adjusted group. They become self-reliant, and enjoy high levels of self-esteem. They strive to be successful and generally achieve their goals. They're socially responsible and generally very happy.

These children enjoy strong and positive relationships with their siblings. Basing their own behaviour on that of their parents, they support and nurture each other and, rather than feeling jealous and competitive, they celebrate the achievements of their siblings. They're loyal to one another and feel proud to be a member of their family. As adults, they'll maintain close contact. In times of need, their siblings are likely to be the first people they ask for help.

Summary

As the Iowa study showed us, as parents we tend to repeat the parenting style we know from our own childhood. That's the easiest thing to do, of course, but it isn't the only possible course of action.

Now that you are aware of the choices you have as a parent, and now that you know the likely consequences of each choice, you're in a position to change things. You can break free of the cycle of parenting as you know it if you wish to do so, and choose instead to raise your children differently, in a way that's more likely to produce the consequences you hope for, both for each of your children individually and also in terms of the way they're likely to relate to each other, as children and for the rest of their lives.

Your own relationships in the family when you were a child

If the way you interact with your children and the way they behave towards one another helps determine their character, it follows that what happened to you in your family of origin has shaped your behaviour – and in particular, your parenting practices.

Your birth order position

If you are the eldest, you're likely to be a warm and nurturing parent. At the same time, however, you may sometimes over-organise and over-direct your children. Middle and youngest children will find this easier to accept than your eldest, although it can mean that they'll develop independence and a sense of their own direction later than they potentially could.

The bigger issue when there's too much 'firstborn behaviour' will be with you and your own firstborn child. You're on course to clash – almost as if you're competing for that role as main carer – even though there's an entire generation between you! This is especially likely between those of the same gender; mothers and firstborn daughters, and fathers and firstborn sons.

If you're a firstborn, it's important that you try to remember to step aside and let your eldest take responsibility for the others, as well as for themselves, at least some of the time, and to reward them for their care and attention. That, more than anything else, will allow the bonds between the firstborn and the others to flourish.

It's hard for any parent to get the right balance between allowing their own firstborn to take charge and help, and encouraging that child to step back so that the others learn to do for themselves – and it's hardest of all for a parent who is a firstborn. However, it's important to try to find that balance. Otherwise, if you give too much responsibility to your firstborn, they may become over-controlling of their siblings and set rigid standards for themselves. If you do all the caring and nurturing, and deny them any chance to join in, not only will the little ones feel over-controlled and perhaps become too passive, but your eldest may become resentful of you. At worst, they may even feel helpless because they don't know how else to earn your praise.

If you're a middle-born, apart from demanding more of your own middle child – or at least thinking that you understand them better than you do the others – you'll value social awareness and social sensitivity above many other qualities.

As long as you don't champion this quality to the exclusion of other values, that's actually a very good thing. It's well established that good social skills are more closely associated with success in adult life than almost any other quality, including academic achievement. When you value this quality, you'll also foster thoughtfulness and empathy, and therefore encourage your children to develop comfortable and close sibling bonds.

If you were the baby of your family, you may unwittingly overvalue quirky or attention-seeking behaviours in your children. Quirkiness and many attention-seeking behaviours are 'cute' and attractive when a child is young. However, when they're older, particularly at the onset of adolescence, it could make them stand out too much from others, and even lead to rejection by their peers as well as their siblings.

Because you were a youngest child, you may also step in too readily, especially with regard to your youngest, when any of them becomes frustrated as they attempt to complete a difficult task. It's uncomfortable to watch any child struggle when you could do the task for them so much more easily, and this is especially difficult for last-born parents because of their own childhood tendency to avoid such discomfort. Instead, you probably reached out for the willing hands that were all around you. However, the only way to allow your children to develop a sense of independence and high self-esteem is to leave them to work out solutions for themselves whenever possible. When you do this, you're also likely to encourage teamwork, thus strengthening the bonds between your children. A balanced approach is best.

Your own birth order position also means you're likely to demand more of the child who shares your birth position, most likely without any conscious awareness of doing so. The reason is that we feel we 'know' what it's like to occupy our own birth position, and, being that much more mature, and believing that we've learned from our mistakes, we want to spare that child from making the same mistakes. This is definitely not a good idea, because we learn far more from our mistakes than we do from having things done for us.

You may also unwittingly favour the child who's in the same birth position that your favourite brother or sister occupies. Similarly, you may find yourself behaving more critically towards the child who shares the same birth position as the sibling with whom you argued most. This is rarely intentional; remember, these patterns are deeply ingrained, and if you don't stop and think, you'll behave just as you did when you were younger.

These are all common tendencies, and they're generally not detrimental. After all, we're not talking about loving one of your children more or less than the others – love is not a measurable quality. But preferring one to another, or regarding one more critically than the others, can lead to resentment, and as a consequence may interfere with the strength of the bonds between them. Your children will thrive most readily, argue least, and develop the most enduring bonds if each one feels you treated him or her as fairly as you do the others. This is, of course, an impossible task! But it's a goal well worth striving for, a goal that calls for enormous amounts of self-awareness.

I hope this section will help you understand your inclinations and tendencies, so that you can change any of them you might wish to alter.

Other ways you influence sibling relationships

There are a number of other factors that affect the quality of the bonds between your children. Several of these – parental divorce or separation, the introduction of step families, moving home, and the presence of a chronically ill sibling or one with special needs – will be discussed in Part 4, Specific Challenges.

Your relationship with each other

You are the role models for your children, so it follows that your own principal relationships – with your partner if you have one, or with any other main carer – will serve as the prototype for your children's relationships with each other, and later on for their relationships with their peers and partners. If you constantly disagree and challenge one another, and if you fail to show respect for the other person's views and opinions, it's highly likely that your children will more often quarrel than enjoy their time together, and more often criticise rather than listen to and support one another.

Try always to present a supportive and united front with your partner or carer when you're with your children.

If you disagree about house rules and methods of discipline, the time to sort out those disagreements and find some sort of compromise is when you're well away from the children – probably best when you're out of the home altogether. When I work with couples who disagree about how best to manage their children, I suggest that they establish a regular 'date night', an evening once a week or once a fortnight when they hire some good childcare and spend the evening together somewhere they both like, somewhere where they can talk through sensitive issues, particularly any disagreements they may have about house rules or parenting practice. It's best to choose a public place, for example a café or restaurant. When we're in a public place, we're much less likely to show inappropriate anger, and instead to work together more calmly to find a constructive compromise..

Your attitudes to work or other obligations outside the home

There aren't many people who are lucky enough to absolutely love their work. However, if you really don't like your job or your caring responsibilities outside the home, or you dislike or resent whatever else takes you out of the house regularly, it's important to try to cast off your negative feelings before you come home.

Park somewhere near where you live, or leave public transport one stop early, and walk the remaining distance home. One of my clients imagines leaving each of the distasteful or overwhelming challenges of her (difficult) job at a particular location along her route home. The next day, and only then, she imagines picking each one back up on her way back into work. This strategy will allow you to leave the cares of work behind, and feel fully able to enjoy your children when you arrive home.

It's important to do so because if you're obviously unhappy at work, it will be hard for your children to understand why you appear to 'choose' to leave them to do something you dislike. This can make them feel less lovable and even lead to lower self-esteem. They're also more likely to offload their frustration and anxiety by arguing with one another.

If, on the other hand, you're obviously delighted to see your children on your return home, and if you're ready to focus fully on what they've been doing in your absence, they won't feel the need to argue with each other, or to compete aggressively for your attention on your return. Knowing they're missed and loved when you're out helps them feel valued, so their self-confidence will increase. As a result, they'll find it easy to be warm and supportive towards their siblings and, when they're in distress, to turn to them for support.

If you leave your children with a carer, be sure to ask them to encourage the children to work together instead of doing everything for them, just as you would. This will ease the transition of care when you return home, and increase the chance that they'll think of their siblings as helpmates rather than as rivals.

Summary

Your behaviour and attitudes towards your children are central to their wellbeing. The type and quality of the relationships they'll develop with each other – and later on with their peers and colleagues – depends largely on you. The parenting style you choose, the way you react to each child, and your attitudes to conflict, problem-solving and responsibility are all critically important. It's vital, therefore, that you consider carefully the values you hope to inspire in your children and the sorts of relationships you wish to encourage. Remember, you weren't born with any of the values, attitudes or behaviours you have now. You learned them all. Therefore, if you wish to change the way you relate to your children, you are free to do so. All you have to do is, first, become aware of your habits, of your automatic responses and ingrained beliefs and attitudes. Second, formulate a clear idea of how you would ideally wish to behave and think. Third, take small steps – maybe one change each week – to reduce the distance between 'you now' and your ideal self.

The more self-confident you appear, and the more often you show how much you genuinely value and respect those you care about, the more likely it will be that your children will grow up confident and socially aware, and that they'll enjoy deep and satisfying relationships with you and with each other.

Part 2

Relationship foundations

6

What does it mean to have a 'good' relationship?

All parents hope that each of their children will find a friend for life – or, even better, several such people. We all want our children to have someone they know will always be there for them, on those occasions when they need help or simply a shoulder to cry on, as well as for the times when they want someone to share their best moments. As parents, we fulfil that role when our children are young. However, an important part of growing up is that a child gradually loosens that dependency on their parents, and begins developing strong relationships with others they can call on as they build a life of their own.

Who could be better to fulfil this role than our siblings? After all, we've known them for longer and shared more important experiences with them than probably anyone else.

In this section, you'll be introduced to the many ways you can nurture your children's relationships and teach them how to sort out problems calmly and effectively, so that they become increasingly able to count on each other for strength and support whenever they need it.

First, however, we need to be clear about what qualifies as a 'good' relationship.

Robert Hinde, who was a professor of zoology at the University of Cambridge, had a long-held interest in the interactions between family members. Throughout his distinguished career, he studied a number of different living creatures, from birds to primates; and later he turned his attention to humans. In 1981 he published a paper entitled 'On Describing Relationships', in which he identified the important components of any relationship, as well as what helps to make it strong, positive and lasting. This definition holds whether we're talking about mother–infant relationships, lovers or friends. You may think this would be an obvious thing to do, but curiously enough, no one before Robert Hinde had set out the principles of a good relationship with such clarity.

He began by defining a relationship simply as 'a series of interactions over time'. The interactions may be one of two types, either 'reciprocal' or 'complementary'. Reciprocal relationships are those in which both individuals engage in the same sorts of behaviours, for example when children build a Lego tower together. Complementary relationships, on the other hand, are those in which the behaviour of each individual is different, but where each behaviour 'completes' that of the other, for example when an older child repairs a toy for a younger child so the younger child can play with it again. Although a relationship may begin either as wholly reciprocal or wholly complementary, over time they usually become a mix of both sorts of interaction.

For a relationship to be considered 'good' – in other words, positive, strong and affectionate – Hinde identified five essential factors.

1. The individuals in that relationship must be able to interact with one another in a number of *different* ways. At various times in its development, the relationship will consist of both reciprocal and complementary interactions, and each individual will fulfil a number of different roles in relation to the other. A good illustration of this is the relationship between an apprentice and their employer. At first, the relationship is complementary – the apprentice needs their employer to guide them every step of the way. However, as time goes on and the apprentice becomes more skilled, the

relationship becomes more reciprocal, and each can help the other in a number of different ways.

2. A good relationship is one that stands the test of time; it must endure even as the individuals within it grow and change. A good example of this is the relationship between a child and their parent.

3. When one person is away from the other for longer than they're used to, one or both individuals will attempt to restore contact. We see this nowadays most often in relationships between good friends.

4. When one of the individuals is anxious or upset, the presence of the other will always help to calm them. Here, of course, the best examples are the relationships between lovers, and those between young children and their parents.

5. Each individual is responsive to the behaviour and feelings of the other – in other words, each individual is 'tuned in' to the other. This factor is what Hinde called 'meshing'.

This last feature, 'meshing', is something that I was fortunate enough to help formulate. Professor Hinde and I had been observing several families (or 'troops') of rhesus monkeys. When the females gave birth, we noticed that some of the babies seemed to grow and thrive wonderfully, and to appear calm and happy, while others in the same troop grew more slowly, and often screamed or in other ways showed signs of agitation and anxiety. We were curious – after all, the conditions in which the monkeys lived were the same for all of the ones we were observing. We wanted to try to find the reason for these differences.

We began by comparing mothers according to their experience of raising babies. This didn't, however, answer our question; some of the less experienced mothers had some of the healthiest, happiest babies, while other older and better-practised mothers continued to produce anxious, timid babies who were often underweight, and who would run to their mothers and beg to be held at the least provocation. Experience clearly was not the key.

Next, we decided to look at how often the babies were cuddled and held by their mothers. This didn't help us much, either – the anxious babies were cuddled just as often as their more easy-going peers.

It was one particular mother–infant pair that finally opened our eyes and allowed us to understand what makes for a contented baby and a calm and happy mother–infant relationship.

Zoe was Rachel's second baby, which meant that Rachel was relatively new to mothering. Nonetheless, Zoe, just as her older brother Clyde had been, was a particularly healthy and calm youngster, more so than any of the other babies born into the troop that year. So we began to watch Rachel and Zoe more closely.

What we discovered was that, although Zoe spent just as much time being held and cuddled as did the other babies, she and her mother seemed to be incredibly well attuned to sensing when that needed to happen. Zoe almost never had to beg her mother for a cuddle. She had only to show that she was becoming distressed, and Rachel would go to her baby straight away and hold out her arms. At the same time, we almost never saw Zoe struggle to free herself from her mother's embrace when she'd had enough comforting and was ready to go back and play with the other monkeys again. Rachel seemed somehow to sense when Zoe was ready, and she'd let her go straight away so the young monkey could rejoin her friends.

Rachel and Zoe's interactions contrasted sharply with some of the other mother–infant pairs. Some of them – those we called the 'indifferent' mothers – were much slower to respond when their babies ran to them, when the baby was clearly quite distressed and begging for a cuddle. These mothers were quite likely to continue what they were doing, scavenging for food or grooming one of the other adults, until the poor baby was literally screaming for their mother's attention. Other mothers – we referred to these as the 'overprotective' mums – would hold their baby in a tight embrace long after the baby had begun to look towards their friends with interest; sometimes long after the baby was clearly ready to explore again. Those babies often had to kick and struggle against their mother before the mother would finally release their little one so it could scamper off and explore once more.

It's not difficult to see the parallels in human interaction. As you'll remember in Part 1 when we talked about parenting styles, parents that Diana Baumrind categorised as 'uninvolved' show behaviour similar to those of the 'indifferent' monkey mothers. 'Authoritative' parents, who set the rules with little regard to their children's individuality, behave in many ways like the 'overprotective' monkey mothers in our troops. In all these cases, the parent and child are 'out of sync' with one another, each failing to recognise and react to what's going on with the other, and what the other needs at any given time.

This sensitivity, this ability to sense more or less immediately what the other individual in a relationship needs and to respond to it appropriately is, I believe, the most important predictor of a good and lasting relationship between any pair of individuals. Robert Hinde called it 'meshing' in the monkeys. In humans that quality is what I call empathy. Empathy is the ability to see things from the viewpoint of the other person, to recognise their needs at that moment, and then to offer appropriate help – not too much and not too little. Almost all humans are born with the *potential* to develop empathy. However, empathy does not enter our repertoire fully formed. This is a quality that must be learned. Therefore, if you want your children to develop good-quality, lasting bonds with one another, the most important skill you'll ever teach them is how to be empathetic.

7

The building blocks for great relationships

1. Be a good role model

As you've no doubt heard many times before, the way you behave will have a far greater impact on your children's behaviours and values than will anything you say to them. 'Do as I say, not as I do' just doesn't work in the long run. You must show your children by example the most sensitive, appropriate and positive ways of interacting with others, ways that obviously leave them – and you – feeling happier and more satisfied.

The best place to start is at home. Whether or not you live with your partner, it's important that your children observe the two of you listening with care and attention to what the other has to say. Before either of you begins a conversation, open with something like, 'Is this an okay time to talk?' This underlines the importance of checking how the other person is feeling, no matter how pressing the issue you wish to discuss.

If it is an okay time, show that you mean it by turning off your screen and by ignoring the phone if it rings while they're speaking. If you give your full attention to the other person, not only will they feel important and valued in your eyes (and therefore wish to continue your relationship), you'll also get through whatever issues need to be discussed more quickly. If that moment isn't a good time to listen, say so! But don't leave it at that. Suggest a time or times that you suit you better.

If the issue is a sensitive one, it's best not to discuss it when either of you is tired, and not in front of others. An excellent technique is to establish the regular 'date night' (see page 76).

FLASHPOINT

Is it ever okay to argue in front of the children? Doesn't it teach them that in real life everyone has disagreements sometimes?

No, I don't think it's helpful to argue in their presence. If parents are clearly in disagreement, their children will either feel frightened because they're no longer sure what 'right' and 'wrong' mean and where the boundaries of acceptable behaviour lie, or they will capitalise on your disagreement and play you off against each other.

The best approach, the one that will allow your children to feel safe and secure and to know where they stand, is always to back each other up when one of you is enforcing house rules, even when the other disagrees – as long, of course, as the children remain safe. Children need firm and clear boundaries to feel secure and to know how to gain parental approval. When they challenge house rules, what they're really doing is testing the clarity and firmness of the rules you set, rather than challenging the rules themselves. When you back each other up, they learn how to cope with limitations. Later on, particularly during the teenage years, they'll feel better able to make their own decisions, even when they're under pressure from their peers to follow the crowd.

At the same time, you have the right to disagree with your partner. Don't, however, show this in the heat of the moment. Once things cool down, perhaps during your next evening out, discuss the disputed rule. Use logic rather than emotional pressure to find a compromise that's acceptable to both of you.

As your children reach adolescence, you'll want to involve them increasingly in setting house rules, so that by the time they leave home they'll know how to establish and stick to a code of conduct of their own (one that's highly unlikely to mirror the one you set them as children, by the way!). Never, however, try to negotiate with them at the time the rules are being challenged.

Another way to demonstrate how to consider the needs and feelings of others is to teach them what therapists call 'accurate reflection'.

Whenever you're trying to understand another person's point of view – your partner, someone you meet while you're out, or the children themselves – ask them to explain further or to clarify what they've said by reflecting it back to them, before you try to come up with a response. You might say, for example, 'Could you explain that in more detail for me, please?' or 'I think what you're trying to tell me is this: ... Am I right?' As always when you're speaking to another person, give them the gift of your full attention – turn your screen off, and remember to make good eye contact.

Always treat people you meet when you're out with kindness and respect. An honest – and it must always be honest – compliment can bring a huge smile to someone's face and leave everyone feeling better. A simple, warm and kindly smile costs nothing, yet it conveys recognition of and respect for others.

When someone behaves inappropriately or says something you disagree with, it won't help to criticise them openly. Unless they challenge you directly, your best approach is what therapists refer to as 'the power of silence'. You can nod or otherwise show you've heard, but say nothing. If you are challenged directly to respond, it's best to reply in a way that shows that you value and have thought through your own judgements but that you recognise that others may hold a different view. For example, you might respond with, 'I hear you, and you're entitled to that opinion, but I can't agree with you.' There's no need to elaborate, and – this may surprise you – if you've thought through your views carefully beforehand, you won't even feel any need to rush to your own defence. We only argue defensively when we're not sure of our view. This approach – recognising the other person's right to their opinion but refusing to abandon your own – demonstrates self-respect, but also shows consideration and tolerance of others.

Of course, what I've just described is the ideal approach when you disagree, and none of us can behave ideally at all times! Therefore, when you do slip up, be sure you show your children that if they become angry and say something hurtful to another person, it's important to make amends. First, apologise to the person you've offended, perhaps with an honest reason why you lost your temper. For example: 'I'm sorry I snapped at you like that. I'm tired today, and I should have held my tongue.'

Second, show your children how to forgive yourself rather than to self-punish or wallow in guilt. Instead, resolve to learn from your mistakes. Feeling guilty is a waste of time, because it's not possible to go back and change whatever it is you regret having said. You can, however, learn from your mistakes and show greater empathy and self-restraint next time.

2. Praise your children

Praise your children when they interact appropriately. When they don't, offer specific and constructive alternatives so that they know what will gain your praise and approval. No child is born knowing the best ways to behave. We all have to learn, and the most reliable way to become socially skilled is to observe appropriate behaviours and then to learn by doing, by copying those behaviours. When parents or other carers are on hand to reward children when they behave appropriately, not only is the experience enjoyable for everyone, but it also means there's less time available for inappropriate behaviour. That's why it's so important that parents – a child's most powerful role models – behave as they hope their children will, and, at the same time, praise their efforts when they're clearly trying to do their best.

However, simply demonstrating good behaviour, even when you also reward your child appropriately, isn't enough to guarantee good social development. Young children are not yet capable of generalising what they've learned. They'll definitely copy – repeatedly – the behaviours you've just rewarded. But they'll also need specific feedback if you want them to generalise what they've learned. So, for example, if your older child asks to help you give the baby a bath, rather than simply accepting their offer, say something like, 'Thank you! It would be great if you help me, because I can't wash her and play with her at the same time. How about if I wash Annie while you make the duck swim in front of her? She loves the duck, especially when it moves, so you'll make her laugh if you do that.' With only a few more words, you've explained things from both your point of view and the baby's, and you've suggested a specific way your older child can please both you and their sister. Everyone gains, and you've introduced the concept of empathy – looking out for what others value.

However, no matter how careful you are to communicate what's appropriate, some inappropriate behaviour is of course inevitable. Here, too, your explanation when you react is crucial.

FLASHPOINT

My toddler snatches toys from my baby constantly. How can I stop him?

Demonstrating a constructive alternative beats criticising or scolding your child – every time. Here's an example. Let's say that your older child is building a tower with blocks, and the baby crawls over and grabs one of the blocks. The older child grabs it back, and the baby starts crying. If you scold your older child – for example, you say, 'Don't snatch that block! Now you've made her cry!' – your older child is likely to feel that your sympathies lie entirely with the baby, not at all with them. After all, it was their block! You've also failed to show them how they could make amends and win your approval. This leaves the older child feeling jealous of their sibling, and powerless because they don't know how to please you. If instead, you were to say, 'Annie shouldn't take your block when you're playing with it, should she? But Annie doesn't understand that it's your block. She likes blocks, too. Is there one of your blocks you could give her while you build your tower? That would be a way of sharing your blocks with her, and maybe that will make her smile again. Do you want to try?' Once again, with only a few more words, you've clarified Annie's viewpoint, and at the same time pointed out her limited understanding of the situation. You've also given your older child a specific coping strategy that empowers them. Now, your toddler knows exactly how they can turn Annie's tears to a smile.

---

3. Talk it through

Make sure there are regular opportunities to talk through the 'small things' so they never grow large. All too often, parents come into my clinic complaining that their teenager won't talk to them. They know something is troubling them, but they don't know what it is or how to find out. This distressing, familiar experience can be avoided if your children grow up thinking it's quite natural to talk things through as they occur.

The way to do this is to establish regular family occasions, times when everyone sits down together without distractions, such as TV or electronic devices, and shares their experiences. To maintain momentum and make it a natural part of your children's upbringing, this needs to happen at least twice a week. The obvious solution is to share some meals together on a regular basis.

Children, and particularly adolescents, are more likely to be forthcoming if they don't feel that others are looking directly at them when they're speaking. This is probably because they become so incredibly self-conscious during adolescence. Whatever the reason, mealtimes are great occasions to talk through things that are bothering children, because the food provides a pleasant distraction, and they needn't look directly at you when they're speaking.

If regular meals are impossible, car journeys (without mobiles or CDs or the radio) are another occasion when children can talk to their parents without having to feel they're being scrutinised directly.

Don't worry if discussions become heated on these occasions – as long as, of course, no one is deliberately cruel to or dismissive of anyone else. Sharing strong emotions, whether these are positive or negative, is associated with establishing closer, more honest relationships between individuals.

Don't be afraid of silence either. Constant questioning is the surest way to close off discussion, especially when you're talking to teenagers. Just let things happen; if you share time together regularly, they will.

When there are disagreements or one child feels they've been treated unfairly, use this as an opportunity to demonstrate empathy. Rather than taking sides or agreeing that something is indeed unfair, ask questions. Use these enquiries to establish first how everyone is feeling. Show your genuine concern if they're upset, and make it clear that their distress is what counts, rather than the particular belief they have. Let's say that at supper one evening, your younger child informs you that their older brother teased them in front of their friends at school. It would be a mistake to react simply by expressing dismay at the older child's behaviour. After all, you've not heard his version of the event yet. For example, he may have no idea that what he said was hurtful. Your first job is to encourage the two of them to understand one another better. A good response in this situation would be: 'Katie, it sounds like you felt really embarrassed when Tom told your friends that you're afraid of spiders. Tom, did you realise that what you said upset her?' This allows Tom the possibility of clarifying – maybe even of apologising – and it helps him be more aware of the effect he has on Katie. If Tom seems genuinely surprised at her reaction, she in turn learns that there can be more than one way to interpret what someone says or does. At the same time, you've validated Katie's distress. Yet throughout, you've blamed no one.

Handling situations in this way – reflecting on what is said, and questioning everyone kindly, with the sole aim of clarifying details – allows you to keep the emotional tone down while at the same time providing each of your children with the chance to be heard.

Regular open, honest communication like this is the surest way to ensure that your children grow up feeling that they truly understand one another. It also shows your children how to negotiate constructively.

4. Provide your children with opportunities to cooperate, not compete

Comparing your children to each other or pitting them against one another means one is bound to feel more inadequate than the other, and it's a sure way to stir up antagonism between them. Instead, praise each for their unique accomplishments, and provide them with as many opportunities as possible to cooperate rather than to compete.

Ask them, for example, to prepare a family meal together. If you have a pet, encourage them to feed it together. Or, as a grander gesture, you could go on a camping holiday and challenge them to set up the tent or gather firewood together.

FLASHPOINT

How do I encourage cooperation between my children in our home?

One of the best ways to do this is to give each child a regular household task – each according to their ability, of course. Be sure to upgrade the tasks periodically. That way, everyone will feel a sense of community, of contributing to home life. At the same time, you're teaching them to be increasingly self-reliant, thus preparing them for independent living later on. Finally, try to set cooperative tasks whenever possible; for example, one child feeds the dog and the other keeps its water bowl filled. Cooperation will deepen and strengthen the bonds between your children.

The importance of cooperation over competition has long been recognised as the best way to create a sense of warmth and closeness between individuals. Probably the most famous psychology experiment comparing these two approaches is what's come to be known as the Robbers Cave experiment. In 1954, the social psychologist Muzafer Sherif assigned a group of 11-year-old boys to one of two groups. The boys were initially strangers to one another, but were all of similar background, and they were assigned to their group by random allocation. Each of the groups then spent one week camping together, away from the other group and unaware of their existence.

After that week, the two groups were introduced to one another and challenged to compete for various trophies. The boys bonded positively with members of their own group. At the same time, however, they became highly antagonistic towards their competitors, the boys in the other group.

Because they were strangers initially, and because the camping experiences were similar for each group, Sherif concluded that these strong emotions were almost certainly due to the incentive to cooperate (which resulted in close bonding) and the instruction to compete (which gave rise to dislike and antagonism).

Pets

One of the most enjoyable ways to foster teamwork as well as a sense of collective responsibility is to introduce a pet – as long as that's feasible, given where you live and how much time you're out at work.

Pets are the perennial babies in a family. They'll always require care and attention, and everything you do for them is met with gratitude. A pet makes a child feel that their efforts are valuable and worthwhile. Stroking the animal, and sharing the responsibility for feeding and caring for it, will strengthen their relationships with one another. The eternal playfulness of most pets will also create some of children's best shared experiences, memories they'll treasure and that will intensify the bonds between them.

One warning: if you do get a pet, be prepared at first to do most of the caring yourself, until you feel certain the children understand what's involved. However, the only way they can feel proud of their contribution is if you delegate aspects of the animal's care once you feel they understand what's expected of them.

5. Allocate your time fairly – not equally

Allocate your time between your children as fairly as you can. Notice that I did not suggest you allocate your time equally. Matching the number of minutes you spend with each child will do little to make them feel they're being treated fairly. Instead, it's vital that you respond to the specific needs of each of them, rather than measuring your interactions in minutes or hours.

Say, for example, that your eldest son has always been a bit clumsy, and has found it difficult to participate in sports although he would very much like to do so. A great way to make him feel special, instead of less adequate than his sporty younger brothers, for example, would be to help him find an all-round, coordination-building sport he enjoys, such as swimming or martial arts – preferably an activity that no one else in the family practices. Then find a class outside school (so he doesn't feel self-conscious among children who already know he has coordination difficulties), and set aside the time to transport him to and from these classes.

To take another example, let's say that your middle son has always been interested in diet and nutrition, and in particular in learning how to prepare healthy foods. You could help him find some appropriate recipes, take him to the shops to buy the ingredients, and encourage him to prepare a meal for the family. Or perhaps your daughter is interested in learning to play the drums. To encourage her and show her how much you want her to explore this interest, you could look for a good drum teacher and rent or borrow a drum kit.

Each of these activities costs different amounts of money and demands different amounts of your time. However, if you treat your children in this way, listening with an open mind to the needs and dreams of each of them, each will feel valued and know that you want to help them feel more fulfilled. They won't feel the need to compare themselves to their siblings, nor will they feel threatened by the skills of the others. Instead of rivalry and jealousy, you're more likely to enjoy observing your children as they develop their talents, and form close and mutually supportive relationships with each other.

The secret is to remember that equal treatment can't be determined by counting up hours and minutes, or pounds and pennies. The key to treating your children truly equally is to respond to the unique needs and desires of each of them, as best you can.

Summary

The five principles presented in this chapter form the basis of my advice when it comes to managing sibling relationships. They are positive activities that will make a difference in your day-to-day family life, and, if followed, will create strong and loving bonds between your children.

8

Understanding sibling rivalry

It may surprise you just how much, and how often, your children seem to compete. From when they were small and arguing over who won a game, and through their school and their teenage years, whenever one of your children is faced with their siblings getting better marks, more prizes, or in some way doing better than they do, that child will redouble their efforts to try to outdo the others. Their aim will be to become the 'best one' in your eyes. This rivalry has the potential to create negative feelings, jealousy and family discord. If left unchecked or responded to thoughtlessly, it can have a lasting effect on the quality of the bonds your children form with one another. This rivalry can also cause you to wonder whether you've done something to bring about this competitiveness, whether you've neglected to teach your children some much-needed life skill, or inadvertently played 'favourites' with one or the other.

Please don't worry. Sibling competitiveness is very normal, a natural part of any sibling relationship. It's not the behaviour itself, but the way you react to it that counts, and you already have some simple guidelines to help you respond helpfully and positively.

Competitiveness is natural

Nature is incredibly clever. Those behaviours that help each species to thrive will continue to show up generation after generation, while behaviours that don't encourage survival soon die away. Given that sibling rivalry has been with us for as long as humans have existed, it follows that the aggressive, competitive behaviours that seem impossible to avoid must help us in some way. How?

Let's start by defining exactly what we mean by sibling rivalry: *Sibling rivalry is the competition, jealousy and animosity among brothers and sisters that begins almost as soon as a second child is born.*

It's important to point out that this sort of behaviour isn't limited to humans. Fierce competition among siblings has been observed in the young of every mammal; in fact, we see this behaviour among the offspring of all creatures who must depend on their parents to care for them when they're very young (birds, for example). The reason we observe this sort of interaction, generation after generation, is that it's absolutely essential for survival when resources are limited.

Every young animal is programmed to grow up to be as strong and healthy as possible, so the more resources that animal can get hold of – the more food, warmth and shelter they can command and enjoy, entirely for themselves – the better off they'll be. Therefore, when a young animal pushes their siblings out of the way in order to eat or obtain warmth, they're simply acting in their own best interests. This is far more important to them than the wellbeing of anyone else, most particularly their siblings, who, after all, are also trying to take all they can of those same limited resources. That's why the weakest baby in a sibling group of animals – for example, the 'runt' in any litter of piglets, puppies or kittens – is likely to be shoved aside. Too weak to push back in to be near its mother, the little creature will almost certainly die unless a human intervenes to feed and care for it. This is the process that allows only the healthiest young of a species pass on their genes.

When we consider human beings, however, the nature of sibling rivalry becomes more complicated than it is in other animals. Of course we need the same basic essentials – food, warmth and shelter – and we'll shove our siblings out of the way mercilessly to get all we can of these resources. Humans, however, need more than the physical essentials in order to thrive. They also need the loving, consistent attention of a parent (or main carer). Babies who don't get the opportunity to form a strong, consistent and loving bond with at least one carer will almost certainly suffer mental health problems later in life. They're likely to be highly anxious and fearful, and they're likely to have difficulties trusting other people or forming close relationships.

Human babies are, therefore, just as hungry to be the 'most special' being ever in their parents' eyes as they are hungry for food. What makes that need even more powerful is, of course, that their parent also supplies the physical resources they need.

I'm sure you can understand now why a child feels so threatened when a new baby arrives, or when one of their siblings achieves something that makes their parents feel incredibly proud of the other child. It's not just their feelings that are hurt. They feel as if their very life is at stake. Dramatic as it may sound, it may help you unpick your child's actions and understand them better.

When your child feels threatened by your focus on another sibling, their behaviour may seem confusing to you. You may notice, for example, that your normally mature, responsible five-year-old appears suddenly to 'regress' when a new baby joins the family. The older child may start demanding to drink from a bottle, even though they know perfectly well how to use a cup. Or they may suddenly start throwing tantrums, a behaviour you were sure they'd grown out of. At other times, they may surprise you by trying to act more grown up than they really are, particularly at times when they know you're watching them.

What's happening is that your five-year-old is trying out different strategies, trying to make themselves appear special to you once more – although of course they're not aware that this is their intention. So on the one hand, they'll see if imitation works, whether behaving just like the object of your new adoration will regain your admiration. They've noticed that babyish behaviours, for example crying piteously or clinging helplessly, make you stop everything else and pay fond attention to the needy child. Hence the regression. Most of the time, not only is this strategy unsuccessful, but it tends to backfire, because parents most often respond by becoming irritated or distressed rather than fondly attentive when an older child appears to go 'backwards'.

So when this strategy fails, the older child may resort to the opposite tactic. Now they'll try to distinguish themselves as much as possible from the baby by behaving like a carer themselves. (Note that these helping behaviours have more to do with self-interest than with any love for the new baby!) This strategy generally has a better chance of success.

However, if neither of these tactics works and the older child still feels ignored or overlooked (in their eyes) by you, their next strategy is to try to eliminate, or at least damp down, the competition. This is when you start to see what most of us think of as typical sibling rivalry – all those aggressive behaviours that can be so distressing to parents.

FLASHPOINT

'You love him more than me!' I get so weary of trying to defend myself to my five-year-old daughter! What am I doing wrong?

A five-year-old (and even children considerably older) does not mean this in the way you are interpreting it. She isn't asking you to weigh up and compare your feelings for each of your children. What a child means when she uses this phrase is 'I'm feeling left out and I want your attention!' And of course it usually works, doesn't it? When your daughter says that, you immediately turn your attention to her.

However, the attention you're giving her is actually aimed at easing your own discomfort more than hers. She probably doesn't want a detailed explanation; what she wants is a cuddle or your full attention.

Next time that happens, try responding like this: 'Sweetie, love isn't something we can measure. Just tell me what's bothering you. Would you like a cuddle? Then after that, how about if you help me make our sandwiches for lunch?' – or something along those lines. This sort of response will give her your attention, but in a positive and constructive way. It also deflects her focus, and minimises the chance that she'll feel jealous of her sibling.

I hope that by understanding better what's going on when siblings appear to be antagonistic, you'll find it easier to accept that 'sibling rivalry' is a totally normal and natural reaction to what a child views as a threat. I hope, too, you'll now find it easier to remain calm and not to feel annoyed when your children behave aggressively towards one another. It's not the other child that triggers their aggression so much as the bottomless desire each one has for your loving care and attention. I'm sure you're already starting, too, to think of innovative ways of looking after each of your children, ways that will not only minimise aggressive behaviour between them, but also nourish a sense of unique identity, and a growing sense of self-confidence and self-pride in each one of them.

What you can do

While sibling rivalry is, as we've seen, a natural phenomenon that is nothing to be worried about, you'll still want to know how to minimise any negative effects on your family, and to ensure that you're not exacerbating an emotional situation. So, for example, if you compare your children to each other or pit them against one another, one is bound to feel more inadequate than the other. This is a sure way to stir up antagonism between them.

Instead, provide them with plenty of opportunities to cooperate rather than to compete, and praise each for their unique accomplishments.

FLASHPOINT

What activities would you recommend to try to help my children get along better?

Look at ways they can work as a team. This can be in a complementary relationship – for example, you ask your older child to read a story to the younger one, or ask the older one to help you give the baby a bath. Or you can encourage them to interact in a reciprocal relationship – ask them to set the table together for a meal, or to play a game or help each other make a card for Granny. Be sure that when they're positively engaged, you let them know how delighted you are, so they learn how to gain your praise and attention.

The more often you can get them to cooperate, the more enjoyable experiences they'll accrue and, as a result, the more positive their feelings towards each other will be.

Summary

In this chapter, you've seen why it's in your children's very nature to compete. You've also learned how to turn this tendency to advantage, instead of allowing it to slide into chronic jealousy and resentment.

We'll continue this theme in the next chapter, and in Chapter 10 we'll look in detail at a specific time when sibling rivalry will certainly crop up – the arrival of a new baby.

9

Dealing with disagreements

Despite all your efforts, your children *will* argue. There will be occasions when at least one of your children has an off day – perhaps they're tired, or they've had a disagreement with a friend or are going through a difficult time at school. When any of us is upset or feels the need to offload anger or resentment, we often do it where we feel safest, where we know we can be at our most unattractive but still be loved. These are the times when your children are most likely to pick an argument with you or with one of their siblings – even though none of you is the cause of their angry feelings.

You may also find that your children are at loggerheads with each other – arguing over possessions, who's turn it is, or whether you are treating them 'fairly'. You may also have a house full of boisterous youngsters who are prone to using their fists to solve arguments. This can be gruelling for parents to deal with.

Here we'll look at what you can do to help relieve tensions in your house before they escalate – and then go into detail as to what to do when an argument is in full swing.

Teach everyone how to 'cool down' when they're feeling upset or angry

Is there anything you can do to make it less likely that your children will butt heads or, if it's already happening, to lower the emotional tone? There is, but you'll need to do some preparation well ahead of time if you want your intervention to make a real difference. Start by teaching them a 'cool down' strategy.

Choose a time when the children are relatively calm and content. Explain that you're going to teach them a way to deal with angry and unhappy feelings, that you're going to show them something that will mean they'll feel okay again, even if they started by feeling really upset.

Before you start, send everyone out to the garden if you have one, or take them to your nearest green space. Explain that each child must find something small but special that they can bring back inside to be their 'lucky object'. The item needs to be something they can pick up and hold easily. The only requirements are that it's a natural object, something that doesn't belong to someone else already, and something they can safely keep in their room; for example, a twig, a pebble or perhaps a leaf, or, if you live near the sea, a seashell. Encourage the older siblings to help the younger ones.

Once everyone has chosen their special object, invite them to bring it with them and come back inside so they can show the others. Explain at this point that the object is something they'll keep by their bed, to remind them to feel calm.

Next, explain to them that whenever we feel angry or upset, the best way to get rid of those horrible feelings is by breathing them away. Then show them how to do this:

- *Breathe in slowly through your nose, counting 1, 2, 3, 4, 5.*
- *Then hold that breath and count 1, 2, 3, 4, 5.*
- *Now breathe out through your mouth, counting 1, 2, 3, 4, 5.*

Practise this all together, and make sure everyone understands how to do it.

Any child who is old enough to understand these instructions is old enough to use this technique. Younger children will count faster than the older ones, and that's fine – just make sure that everyone counts to five every time, so that each feels as 'grown up' as the others.

Now, you can say, they know the secret of the 'calm breath'. Now, whenever they feel upset, if they remember the breathing and do it straight away for ten breaths, they'll feel calmer again. Practise it a few more times.

Finally, explain that if they do the ten breaths while holding and looking at their special object, they will feel even better. This is because the object is natural, and Nature 'knows how to be calm'. In addition, of course, their object will quickly become associated with a shift from agitation to greater calm. This is because a familiar object, something that's used for one purpose and one purpose only, what psychologists refer to as a 'cue', 'triggers' the appropriate feelings more quickly. Depending on the ages of your children, you may or may not wish to add this more complicated additional explanation.

That's all you need to do in preparation, although it would be a good idea if you all practised the ten breaths several times during every week. You could do it with each child at bedtime one evening, or all together just before a meal once a week. Encourage the children to keep their special object in a safe place in their bedroom.

Start to notice 'hot spots' so you can intervene before an argument starts

You've just helped your children create an environmental cue that will, with practice and repeated association, allow them to calm down quickly whenever they're feeling distressed. Unfortunately, there are already a number of other cues in their environment that will have the opposite effect – things that will make them much more likely to become angry and argumentative. Some of these are internal, for example if they're tired, if they have low blood sugar, or – when they're older – if there's a sudden hormonal shift. Other triggers are external; when you get out their school uniform at the end of August, for example, they'll know it's almost the end of the summer holidays and time to live a more prescriptive life. Or the end of a particular TV programme means that it's time to get ready for bed. If you can learn to identify these triggers, you may be able to avoid, or at least be prepared for, a great deal of argumentative, grumpy interactions.

You can probably identify some of your family's triggers already. Make a list of the obvious 'bad mood triggers', and beside each, make a note of what you could do to avoid or lessen a negative reaction. Keep your list handy, and keep your eye out for more triggers.

Once you've identified one of these, the best approach is either to eliminate it altogether if you can or – if things have already started to heat up – to distract everyone by giving them a cooperative task or suggesting some 'own time'. Here are some examples.

Let's say you know that your middle child, a fussy eater, often refuses to eat all his school lunch. As a consequence, by the time he arrives home from school, he's hungry. This is an internal cue, and it means he's likely to arrive home feeling angry and irritable. His first reaction may be to pick an argument with his little sister. To avoid this, you could take a healthy snack with you (or with whoever is picking him up from school) that he can enjoy as soon as he comes through the school gates on the way home. If his younger sister is with you when you pick him up, be sure to provide a snack for her to have at the same time, so that both of them feel they've been treated fairly.

A typical 'external' trigger is bedtime. Let's assume that your spirited youngest child thinks it's unfair that she has to go to bed first, so when 7.30 comes round she prepares to argue with anyone she can, to delay her bedtime. In this situation, try offering a reward for cooperative behaviour. For example, tell her that if she's ready for bed by herself by 7.30, then she can stay up until 7.45 and listen to a bedtime story read to her by her big brother. In this way, not only are you offering the little one an incentive to behave maturely, you're also providing an opportunity to praise her brother for helping you entertain his little sister.

FLASHPOINT

It seems like no matter how hard I try to treat my two fairly, the younger one accuses me of favouring his older brother. What can I do about this?

No doubt your little one is probably comparing what he is allowed to do in relation to the 'privileges' his older brother enjoys, and is feeling jealous of what he's being allowed even though it's appropriate for an older, more mature individual. You can begin by pointing out encouragingly that he, the younger one, will be allowed these privileges just like his brother when he reaches a similar age.

Meanwhile, what the little one is also trying to tell you is that what he's currently allowed doesn't feel particularly special to him.

Why not take him out, just the two of you, to his favourite eating establishment, and while you're enjoying a meal together, ask him to name a specific privilege he'd like to have. If it's not appropriate right now, suggest something you do feel comfortable offering. Present them to him as what psychologists call a 'forced choice' decision. For example, if he says he wants to stay up until 8 p.m. like his brother, but he currently has a 7 p.m. bedtime, offer him a choice of two new situations. Either he can stay up until 7.15 every evening, or he'll be allowed to stay up until 8 p.m. like his brother, but only on Friday and Saturday nights. That way, he'll feel he's made a real gain either way, and at the same time, you'll be happy with either of the options you've offered. Make the offer with a proviso: if he is unpleasant or reluctant to go to bed at the new times when asked to do so, he loses the new privilege.

This is a problem similar to 'You love him more than me' (see page 100). What you need to do here, as in that case, is to consider the meaning behind your younger son's words, rather than to react to what he says at face value. In this case he is asking to be treated as more grown up, like his brother. Respond to this by offering him something he must prove he's able to handle with maturity.

Finally, let's imagine that it's too late to avoid triggers. You've heard sounds that suggest an argument has already started between your two older boys. They each want to watch a different sports match – both are on at the same time – on your widescreen TV. Your best strategy in this situation is to distract them from arguing with one another, and turn their attention to you. Tell them that neither can watch their chosen programme because there's only one big TV and it can't show two programmes at once. Suggest instead that they each watch their chosen match on their own devices. This gives them a 'time out' from arguing, and 'permission' to retreat to their own space without losing face. Furthermore, because you treated them equally and at the same time eliminated the reason for any competition, they're also likely to forget the resentment they felt towards one another quite quickly.

Now, they may turn any residual irritation away from one another and towards you. That's OK – as long as you remain calm and firm. Whereas, only a moment ago they were angry with each other, they're now likely to feel supportive as they each 'endure' the equal 'deprivation' you've imposed on them.

FLASHPOINT

My children constantly call each other names, and tease each other. I get so agitated! Is this normal behaviour for two boys close in age?

This is an interesting problem, because in truth, I suspect this is an example of sibling *cooperation* rather than sibling rivalry! The two of them, it seems, have learned how to work together to gain your attention.

Start by thinking about your own behaviour. When the boys are settled and cooperative, do you breathe a sigh of relief and turn to something you want to do for yourself? Do you continue until you hear them arguing, then go to them in distress?

If so, you are in effect rewarding the arguing and ignoring the behaviour you really want! Therefore, whenever they're cooperating, you need to give them some praise and attention. When they argue, on the other hand, separate them immediately, without scolding or showing that you're upset. Tell them they can come back together as soon as they've thought of a way to get along. (This may take some time at first!) When they're calm and behaving well, praise them, and perhaps offer them both a privilege – going to a film at the weekend, for example – as a reward for being so nice to each other.

This is a big ask, I know, because it means that for now, you may end up with less time to do the things you want to do. It may mean you have to rethink your usual habits and routines, to find time for yourself more often when the boys are at school or in bed. But this is a relatively short-term investment, and one that will pay excellent long-term dividends!

Finally, think carefully about how you respond to other people, especially when you're feeling uncomfortable or bored. Do you 'tease' others? Teasing is close to insulting. It's a way of releasing aggression, and it can be very hurtful. Perhaps you need to react to other people in a kinder, more compassionate way, especially in front of your children.

What to do when an argument is already in full flow

If you become aware of an argument only when your children are in full flow, it will be too late to avoid high emotions. Try to curb your initial reaction of dismay or guilt! No parent can pre-empt every disagreement, and if you watch them all the time, they may resent your apparent refusal to trust them. Instead, think of this argument as an opportunity for them to learn how to solve an interpersonal problem, to find ways to reach a compromise that's acceptable to both of them. As long as it sounds like no one is in danger, simply listen unobtrusively. Try to allow them to find a way to settle their differences themselves.

If, however, things only seem to be getter more and more bitter, or if one or both children is actually in danger (physically or emotionally), you'll have to step in. This is where your preparation with the breathing technique and the special object will pay off.

Confront the two of them, and tell them, calmly but clearly, that you feel things have gone too far. At the same time, make it clear that you are not blaming either of them. Tell them you don't want to hear about the argument yet, that you only want to listen when everyone has calmed down. Therefore, both must go to their rooms to pick up their special object and practise a double session of breathing – 20 breaths while holding the object. (If they share a room, you'll need to ask one or both of them to do this exercise somewhere else, so they're out of sight of one another.) Afterwards, invite them to come back in with you. If they're still not settled, ask them to go back and do another set of 20 breaths.

Once everyone is reasonably calm, ask each to explain why they're angry with the other, what they feel has gone wrong. Listen without comment, and tell them that the other child is not allowed to interrupt the one who's speaking.

Next, ask each to describe what the problem is *from the point of view of the other child*. This is hard, especially for anyone under five, and it may be that only one of them is able to do this, even with helpful questions from you. However, encourage both to try. As before, each child is not allowed to interrupt or criticise the other. Stepping outside their own point of view in this way will encourage the development of empathy and help bring the two of them closer together again.

Now it's your turn. Reflect what you think each child is feeling, and how each sees the problem. Ask if you've got it right, and correct yourself until everyone agrees that you're describing the situation accurately.

You now need to ask each child to suggest *two* potential solutions, *two* ways to solve the disagreement. This introduces the idea of compromise, as opposed to 'winning' and 'losing'. Stay as neutral as you can – blaming won't help – and keep encouraging them to think and suggest, until they arrive at an acceptable compromise. Finally, help them translate this compromise into specific behaviours.

Getting your children to work together in this way takes considerably more time than simply stepping in and sorting things out yourself. But it's well worth it, because what they'll gain is priceless. They'll become more adept at and confident about solving interpersonal problems. You'll have created circumstances in which you can praise them rather than berate them. And best of all, you'll have encouraged each to learn a bit more about their sibling and, as a result, you're helping them to develop an increasingly close and strong relationship.

FLASHPOINT

My children always fight physically. It's more than rough and tumble, and it's worrying me. What can I do?

With this problem, you'll need to take the long view.

Start by looking out for 'hot spots', occasions when the children are more likely to feel angry or irritated, and for 'cues', things that ramp up frustration, such as low blood sugar after participating in sports. Look for ways to avoid or, if that's not possible, to defuse them. For example, in the case of the low blood sugar, have a tasty and nutritious snack ready as soon as they arrive home from their sports activity.

Second, think honestly about the way you and their other parent react to frustration. Are you good role models, calm and reasonable, or do you lash out? You may need to change your own behaviour before you can expect your children to change theirs. You are, after all, their most important role models.

If you are calm and reasonable, could it be that you're allowing them to watch too much violence on screen? You may have to limit their intake of such material. Couple that, however, with examples of more adaptive ways of behaving, both through your own example and by taking them to see good films, or permitting less violent screen viewing in place of what you've banned or limited.

Finally, think of other, more positive ways to encourage them to release energy. For example, ask if they'd like to learn karate or judo or some other martial art. These disciplines encourage children to be assertive – confidently aware of their own abilities and worth – as opposed to aggressive – angry and overly forceful. Martial arts also encourage concentration, focus and reflection, so children learn to stop and assess a situation before acting. This is particularly helpful for those who tend to be impulsive. You might also ask if they'd like to try participating in drama classes. There are a number of organisations that offer drama courses if your school doesn't do so, and meeting other children who might become new friends would also help them feel more confident socially.

Note: Once everyone has cooled down after an aggressive outburst, it's best simply to suggest or encourage, and then praise, more acceptable behaviour, rather than trying to rehash the dispute or impose punishment. Punishment teaches only one thing, and that is to avoid being caught again. Punishment does not teach adaptive behaviour. You need to do that, by example, by offering specific suggestions, and by praising what you wish to see.

Summary

The key to dealing with disputes and disagreements is to teach and reinforce how to resolve issues adaptively, both by example and by repeated specific suggestions. Overall, build on what you want your children to do and say, so there's less and less time for negative behaviour. This, more than any sanction or punishment, will help them feel good about themselves and more positive towards one another. It will also teach them how to get on well, not just with their siblings, but with everyone.

Part 3

Living with siblings

10

Introducing a new baby

The introduction of a new baby is often a worrying time for parents. With one or more older siblings, parents brace themselves for outbursts of jealousy towards the baby and worry how the older ones will cope with less attention from their parents. Here we'll look at how you can ease your family through this transition, and what to do should problems arise. Know that while this can be a hard time for young children, they are gaining a sibling – someone to play with and hang out with for years to come. It may be a turbulent time at the start but very soon your child will not remember life without their younger sibling.

Can you prepare your child emotionally?

As adults, we often assume that our children understand the world much as we do, that they can anticipate time accurately and imagine what is to come realistically. They can't. Each of us sees 'reality' in our own individual way, according to our particular needs and desires, and to complicate matters further, when we're young we have a limited understanding both of time and of other people's viewpoints.

Until they're about six or seven, children generally assume that everyone sees the world exactly as they do, according to their own current needs and desires. They find it challenging to consider the ways things might appear from anyone else's point of view. Their concept of time is also unlike that of an adult. 'Now' is really all that counts, although they're aware of the past, but not necessarily in its sequential order. The future, on the other hand, is extremely vague and amorphous, a place where 'change' has very little meaning and fantastic possibilities seem as likely as realistic ones.

This is why you don't need to feel too concerned about preparing your child 'properly' for the arrival of a new sibling. Prepare them practically by all means (we'll look at how you might do that in a moment). Otherwise, simply make sure they know that a big change is afoot, and do tell them what that change will be, *from their perspective* – 'You're going to be a big brother/sister!' But there's no need to try to explain repeatedly exactly what that might mean, because they simply cannot envisage the future as you do. Answer their questions honestly, and watch their face carefully to know when you've said enough on each occasion.

Meanwhile, take really good care of yourself, rest when you can and eat well so that you remain as positive, rational and cheerful as possible, because children pick up on parents' moods more powerfully than they do on what parents tell them – and when things seem bad, they're quite likely to assume that they did something wrong to upset you. Other than that, however, the work you'll need to do to maximise the chance that your children welcome the new arrival will really only start once the new baby arrives.

Practical preparations

There's a great deal you can do in practical terms to ensure that your children will accommodate the new arrival easily, and cope with the birth as well as possible.

First, before you introduce the new baby to your other children, try to have as much as you can ready at home. In particular, make sure the other child/children are used to sleeping where they'll be sleeping, so they don't feel suddenly displaced when the new baby arrives.

Make sure, too, that they're familiar with whoever will be looking after them while you give birth. If, for example, they're going to stay with their grandparents, or their grandparents are coming to stay, have at least one trial run before you give birth, so that this doesn't feel like a totally foreign experience to them. This is especially important if you know you're likely to have to stay in hospital for a few days – if you're planning to have a Caesarean birth, for example.

Prepare yourself for life with several children by putting together a box (or boxes) of activities for the older ones to dip into – a book of jokes, some stories, some soft toys, perhaps some games. The children can help you put these together, but the boxes are not to be opened until the new baby comes home. When the baby does arrive, you can get these prepared boxes out, so your children have something rewarding and entertaining to keep them busy when you must attend to the baby. That way, they'll come to associate the baby with positive, special things.

Finally, when you pack your bag for the hospital (if that's where you'll give birth), be sure to include at least one photo of the other child/children, and/or some of their drawings or written work. Pack this item ostentatiously in their presence, so they know you'll be thinking about them.

Meeting the new baby

Whether your other child/children first meet the new baby in hospital or whether it's at home, their initial meeting is important. Although none of them is likely to retain a clear memory of exactly what happened during that first encounter (unless there are siblings who are considerably older, over about seven years of age), the emotional tone of that first encounter will set the stage for future interactions.

Arrange the timing so that just before everyone meets up, you've fed and changed the baby. That way, your littlest one is likely to be contented, and you'll be able to focus your attention on the others. If you're arriving home, have someone else carry the baby in if at all possible, so that your arms are free to hug the others. These small gestures are so important! They allow you to convey, from the start, that all your children are incredibly important to you, and although you've been attending to the baby, you're right there, ready at the first possible moment to show them how much you love them, too.

If any of your children appears cool or indifferent, try not to show that you're hurt or put out. Some children deal with the distress of a separation by rejecting the returning parent initially. It's almost as if they're afraid to appear needy and vulnerable, in case you go away again. The less notice you take of this the better, so the child doesn't think that such behaviour will gain them your attention. At the same time, keep an unobtrusive eye out for when you could hug them in a way that would feel natural but not controlling.

Similarly, don't feel offended if one of them appears to regard the baby as quite a boring creature, not long after the initial meeting and greeting. This isn't a bad sign – quite the contrary. It means that your children are sensing that it's okay to express their honest feelings. Some children are not particularly interested in (helpless) babies. However, as long as they don't feel pressure to pretend to like the new arrival, they're very likely to take an interest in them later. By being accepting and patient, you'll avoid a great deal of resentment.

It's often suggested that a gift from the new baby to each of their siblings will increase the chances that the older children will greet the new arrival more favourably. I'm not sure how long such feelings would last, but there's certainly no harm in making this gesture. Younger siblings will just enjoy the gift, but the older ones – well aware that a tiny baby could not actually have chosen a gift for them – will ask you about it. As ever, answer honestly and positively – perhaps something like this: 'You're right. Really, I chose this gift. But I did it because I know how lucky our new baby is to have you as their brother/sister.' Any explanation that features the benefits the baby offers to the older siblings, rather than the other way round, is most likely to make them feel positively disposed towards the new arrival.

The first few weeks

Start as you mean to go on. The golden rule for ensuring good relationships now as well as later on is always to try to see things from the older children's point of view.

Let's take an example. Once you're back home with the baby, all your children will want your attention, particularly the young ones, and most particularly if they're not used to being separated from you.

Because predictable timetables will not be possible for some time to come, focus on what you can do to reassure each of the others, when they ask, that you're there for them, too. Don't try to control the times when you reassure them each day – instead, respond to their needs as and when they arise.

Choose one activity that each child really enjoys – a bedtime story, a bath, telling you what happened at school that day – and find a way to make that happen every day, just you and that one child sharing special time together. This is so important, because if each of your children still feels valued and knows that you recognise what matters to them, you'll give them little reason to resent the new baby. This can be a real challenge – it's so much easier to promise yourself you'll do this when things 'settle down'. But by then, the resentment will have started to grow. Remember, it doesn't matter how brief the exchange is. The key is that something positive, predictable and special happens between you and each of your children, every day.

Try, too, to say goodnight to each child individually, without bringing the baby with you. You give reassurance beyond measure if you share the last moment of each day with each of your little ones. This will be much easier if you stagger their bedtimes.

In an attempt to regain a sense of focus, you may consider putting each parent, or whoever else is helping you, in sole charge of a particular child. Please don't do this! It makes children feel that they've been overlooked by whoever is not their carer, particularly because they've almost certainly been accustomed to being cared for by either you or your partner or both, at least to a major extent, in the past. This is another thing that might make the new baby appear to be a threat, someone who is taking over Mum's or Dad's attention. Better to make sure that each main carer spends some time with each child, hopefully during those activities they shared with that child before the new baby arrived. So, for example, if Dad always took Olivia to Gymtots, try to ensure that he still does so. If Mum always does the bedtime baths, stagger bathtimes so that she can still do that, while Dad or Grandma looks after the baby.

If there's no one around to entertain the others while you feed the baby, then before the next feeding time, prepare a tempting snack – some slices of apple with raisins, for example, or half a peanut butter sandwich – for the others, so that everyone feels they're being fed. This is just another little way to emphasise that you believe all your children are worthy of equal treatment.

One other easy way to avoid jealous feelings, which will benefit the baby as well as the other children, is to use a sling to carry the baby around. Check with your midwife or GP if you're in doubt about which slings are most comfortable to wear and at the same time are guaranteed to be safe for you both. If possible, carry your baby so that he or she faces you, so that they can see you and feel the warmth of your body. This is the most natural way to reassure the baby of your presence, the position that will allow them to feel safest and most secure. This position, referred to as 'ventral-ventral' by animal behaviourists, is the position that most higher-mammal mothers use to carry their babies around with them in the early days after birth. It has the added advantage of freeing both your arms, so you're better able to meet the needs of the other children, as well as your own.

Finally, before visitors arrive to meet the latest member of your family, ask them to consider bringing a small gift or token for each of the other children. This is a more valuable gesture than bringing a gift for the baby, because the others will feel 'centre stage' again when a visitor arrives, rather than jealous of the attention-stealing newcomer. Ask them as well if they would greet the other child/children first, before asking to see the latest arrival.

'Helping' behaviours

There's no evidence to suggest that if you encourage your older children to help care for the baby, they will bond more closely with them. In fact, your requests may have the opposite effect: afraid of losing your favour, a child may well respond with caring behaviour, but at the same time, underneath, they'll be feeling less valued as a unique and interesting individual. It may seem to them that they're simply being treated as an extra pair of hands to nurture the precious new child, instead of an important person in their own right. You know your children, and you'll know which ones are more interested in young creatures and in developing caring skills, and which would rather play games with their sibling or share adventures with them when they're older. If you want good, positive, lifelong relationships to develop between your children, your best bet is to look out for the ways each child most enjoys relating to the others and encouraging those behaviours, rather than imposing a 'one size fits all' approach on all of them.

That said, whenever one of your children does help with the baby, frame your praise wisely, in a way that suggests that not only you, but also the baby, is pleased. So for example, you might say, 'Holding the new nappy for me until I needed it really helped Sammie feel more comfortable again. Look how she's smiling now. She's so lucky to have you for her big brother/sister!'

Finally, a reminder about helping behaviours: it's great when children want to learn to nurture and when they enjoy helping others. However, if a child starts to think that this is the only way they'll gain your praise, they may decide that their self-worth is only defined in terms of helping other people. If that happens, then later on, particularly in adolescence, it will be difficult for them to develop a unique sense of identity. Try to remember to praise them for their own achievements and self-expression as well for their nurturing skills, for example by noting their achievements at school: 'Harry, you brought home the most wonderful drawing from school today! This is beautiful! Let's put in up in the kitchen so everyone can see it.'

Aggression and regression

No matter how hard you try, it will be impossible to avoid all jealousy when a new baby arrives. After all, your time is finite, and no matter how skilfully you try to balance your attention, there's still 'less of you' to go around now that there's another child in the family! Remember, you are the most precious resource your children have.

The most common ways an older child will express jealousy of the new baby is either to make it cry, or to show some regressive behaviour – in other words, to behave in more 'baby-like' ways. This makes sense from their point of view; if you seem to pay most attention either to those who cry or to the most helpless, they may conclude that they can best get your attention if they produce some tears, or behave more like a helpless baby themselves.

FLASHPOINT

My toddler is very aggressive towards my baby – he's hit and pinched him. What can I do?

When an older child pinches the baby or snatches a toy, or in some other way deliberately makes the baby cry, your natural reaction is to round on the aggressor. You feel your instincts kick in and the desire to protect your baby means that you may shout at your older child, and show them how angry you are. This isn't, however, the best approach. Your older child was not only releasing aggression, but also seeking attention. If you scold them, you'll only encourage them to repeat that behaviour, because in effect you're rewarding them with your attention – even though it's negative attention, it's still better than no attention as far as they're concerned.

A better approach is to rush to the baby and soothe it, without blaming the older child, but also without giving the older child any attention. Then later – a couple of minutes later, so your approach doesn't seem to be linked to the 'attack' – have a word with your older child. 'You seem out of sorts, James. Is there something we could do together that would help you feel better?' You'll now have to keep a more watchful eye on the children's interactions lest the older child tries to test you again. However, if you react consistently and in this manner, things should settle down quite quickly.

It can be really upsetting for you if your older child behaves aggressively toward the baby, and you may be surprised by the strength of your anger toward your older one. You may also feel guilty – that by having a new baby you've caused your child to feel insecure about your love for them. Please don't feel guilty! This is your child's natural reaction to this new and incomprehensible situation. If you take a few deep breaths and follow the advice in the Flashpoint above, you should soon see a positive change in their behaviour.

If your older child shows their frustration by 'identifying' with the attention getter – by acting like a baby themselves – they'll feel they got it right if you give them lots of attention for a tantrum or for wetting their pants, or for whatever else they do to become more baby-like. Instead of making a fuss, simply make sure they're safe, clean any mess, and treat the entire incident in a totally matter-of-fact manner, as if their behaviour is unworthy of attention or note.

At the same time, be on alert for any age-appropriate behaviours, and praise those richly – even if you know your older child has been capable of these behaviours for some time. For example: 'Richard, I'm so proud of you for putting on your shorts and T-shirt all by yourself this morning! You really are a big boy!' Follow this with some extra cuddles whenever possible.

When these negative behaviours fail to achieve the intended aim of parental attention, they'll die away. Furthermore, when instead your older one demonstrates positive, mature behaviours and you praise them lavishly, you'll begin to see more and more 'grown-up' behaviour, which you can remind them is showing the baby how to behave when they grow up.

Sowing the seeds of good relationships

Thus far we've concentrated on helping each child feel valued so that jealousy and aggression towards the new baby are less likely. However, there's more to a strong bond than a lack of negative feelings! So what can you do specifically that will encourage the creation of positive and lasting bonds between your children?

Empower the older child

Teach your older children how to make the baby laugh and smile. This is more important even than teaching them to help, because joy is equally rewarding to both. For example, show your older one how to play peek-a-boo with the baby, or point out toys they can offer that are guaranteed to make the little one smile.

Teach empathy

Empathy is the ability to understand, share and react appropriately to the feelings of others. Nothing is more likely to ensure a close relationship between your children than if each learns to become empathetic. There's a wider advantage, too. Empathetic children are more likely to be popular with their peers and happier at school. The way to teach empathy is to point out emotional expressions to your older child and explain what each one means. Remember, they'll engage with you more readily if you describe things from their point of view or in ways that are advantageous for them. For example, you might say, 'Look, Ruby's smiling! She smiled as soon as she heard your voice. I really think she knows that you're her big brother now and that makes her happy.' Or you could say, 'Ruby's crying. What do you think is wrong? What do you think we could do to help her feel better?'

Establish traditions

The sooner you start to establish family traditions and the more often you repeat them, the more likely it is that your children will remember doing things together. These traditions will also serve as a great anchoring point when siblings get together again when they're grown up. For example, you could share a particular meal once a week – Sunday night is spaghetti night, for example. A 'backwards day' every so often is another great idea. Everyone starts the day with a bath and supper, followed by lunch, and ending with breakfast.

Summer holidays can also become traditions. A camping holiday in Wales, or an annual week in Cornwall in the same cottage will be fondly remembered, even – perhaps particularly – when things don't go as planned, or it rains every day one year. And of course there's the fun of establishing traditions at Christmas and other holidays – who serves the pudding, who distributes the gifts, etc.

FLASHPOINT

My older child has told me he hates his new sister and wishes she'd never been born. How should I react?

Once again, it's important to respond to the underlying message rather than taking what your child says at face value. What he's trying to tell you is more about himself than about his feelings for the baby. The message is: 'I'm missing the way life used to be. I feel left out and unimportant.'

Therefore, you need to do two things. First, re-establish a daily 'special time' with your older child, something you did together (exclusively) before the baby came along, such as reading him a bedtime story or giving him his bath. Make sure the baby is settled or that someone else cares for them while you spend this special time together.

Second, find ways to make the baby seem more of a help than a hindrance in terms of gaining your older child some of your positive attention. For example, teach him how to make the baby smile by making the baby's mobile move, or putting on some special music, or helping you give the baby a bath. Praise him lavishly, while ignoring any negative comments.

Summary

The arrival of a new baby in your family will call for big adjustments, and no doubt it will mean that you're in for many disturbed nights and unpredictable days as well. Remember, however, that the disruptions and disturbances will not last.

It's important to think not only about how to deal effectively with any rivalry and jealous feelings you notice between your children, but also about how to ensure that there are plenty of opportunities for them to bond more closely. Use some of the suggestions in this chapter to help you achieve both of these important aims.

When you bring another unique personality into the family, you're guaranteeing richer, more diverse interactions, and you're providing a wider base of support and friendship among your children. The hard work will be well worth your efforts!

11

School life

The same or different schools?

In 2015, the UK schools minister pledged to give siblings the automatic right to attend the same state school. His intention was not to ensure that siblings have the best chance of forming strong and lasting relationships, of course. His aim was to ease the burden on parents, so that they wouldn't have to drop off their children at two, sometimes even three, different schools more or less simultaneously, while also ensuring that they themselves arrive at work at a reasonable hour.

Despite the fact that his intentions didn't centre on sibling bonding, the minister's pledge raises some important considerations. Is it best, both for each child as well as for their relationships with one another, that all the children in your family attend the same school, or for younger siblings to have the same teachers that their older sister or brother had? Or is it better that each has different teachers, to minimise the chance that they'll be compared, or that younger children will be expected to achieve to the same level as their older sibling?

Before answering these questions, we need to consider the all-important first step, which is to find the school that is most suitable for the family as a whole. In Chapter 20 on giftedness, we make a distinction between treating each of your children 'fairly' as opposed to 'equally'. Some children may need particular help or facilities to allow them to overcome a learning difficulty, for example assigning a tutor to help a child who is severely dyslexic. Other children are more likely to flourish if there are certain facilities that allow them to express an outstanding gift – a sports playing field or an outstanding gymnastics coach, for example. Obviously, one way to deal with this is to find classes and tutors outside school. However, not many parents have the time or the funds to take this route, at least exclusively.

The reality is that most siblings attend the same school. Many schools have a policy that as younger siblings enter the school, they are taught by the same teacher as their elder siblings. This, while trying to ensure a sound knowledge of each family, can bring with it some challenges for parents.

Teachers' expectations based on older children's qualities

Has one of your children excelled in a particular way? Conversely, does one have a learning difficulty that requires them to have extra help? That child's teacher, without realising it, may have formed expectations about your other children, and may assume that they will have similar talents or face similar challenges. You may, for example, have a very sporty eldest child, a child who is best in his class at football and always the first one across the line in sports day. Along comes your more studious younger child, who struggles with the expectation that he will follow in his older brother's footsteps. His lack of natural sporting ability, while totally normal, will be highlighted so much more because of his brother's abilities.

There's also a possibility that your children will be 'lumped together' and lose some of their individual identity. The 'Smith sisters', who are overly boisterous at playtime and talk during assembly, for example, may tarnish your third child's reputation before she's even started at school. While teachers do their best to get to know every child individually, it's also human nature to make associations.

If you suspect this may happen at your school, do talk to the head teacher to see if it would be possible for the younger child to have a different year teacher. That way, they'll have a better chance to express their individuality and develop their particular strengths and talents. This will also mean that younger children are less likely to resent their older sibling, who, through no ill intentions, has set a 'standard' for the family.

If one of your children has special needs, you may also need to ask teachers at your children's secondary school to be particularly sensitive if, as part of their difficulties, they exhibit bizarre or embarrassing behaviours. Adolescents feel particularly sensitive – and they will be especially vulnerable to teasing and rejection by their peers. Therefore, if they have a sibling who behaves oddly, no matter how much they love that sibling, they'll feel distressed and embarrassed about their unusual behaviour. If teachers are aware of this, they will know to be careful not to make comparisons or to ask a sibling to help out with the child who has special needs, particularly in front of the other children. This sensitivity will mean that the siblings are more likely to remain on good terms. This is particularly valuable for a child with special needs, who may not have many other companions.

Pre-existing nurturing bond between siblings

In some situations it will benefit both children if one does follow closely in the footsteps of another – in other words, if they do both have the same year teachers. Cheti Nicoletti and Birgitta Rabe at the University of Essex found this to be the case, particularly when the older child has a good academic record and enjoys helping their younger siblings. The researchers compared the academic performance of younger and older siblings at secondary school. They found that the younger children benefited greatly from an academically successful older sibling when they had the same teachers. No doubt the 'Pygmalion effect', which is explained in Chapter 20, is acting here to some extent. Nicoletti and Rabe also found that the younger child performed better when their older sibling helped them with homework, when the older sibling passed on information to their younger brother or sister about who were the most inspiring teachers and which were the most interesting classes, and when the younger sibling considered their older brother or sister to be an important role model. These benefits were magnified when English was not the family's first language, and if the family income was low.

It seems that when an older sibling does well academically, under the right conditions the younger members of the family may feel more encouraged also to do well. Although the authors of this study did not report on this, I suspect that such cooperation also strengthens the relationship between these sibling pairs.

When one child is gifted

In Chapter 20, we consider the best ways to foster sibling relationships when one child has an outstanding gift or ability. This is one situation – and it's a relatively rare occurrence – when you may wish to consider sending your children to different schools. You should seriously consider this if there is a particular school that would encourage the gifted child to develop their talent.

At the same time, sending them to different schools would allow the other children in your family to flourish in their own way, rather than to be compared to a child whose talent has probably already been clearly noticed.

Although it is possible that younger children in your family would benefit from the example and help given by an older, particularly talented sibling, as was shown in the Nicoletti and Rabe study (see page 129), in reality this is unlikely to work well when the older child is not just able, but truly gifted. That's because, unless their sibling has a similar gift, they're unlikely to come near to achieving the same level of performance as the older one in that area. It would therefore be unfair and unrealistic to expect this to happen. Nonetheless, at the same school and with the same standards applied to both children, it would be hard for the younger child to avoid thinking that they should match their older sibling's ability, and that if they don't, others around will be disappointed in them.

There's a second reason as well why it's unrealistic to expect a gifted sibling to help. If that child has chosen to develop their talent as far as possible, it would be unreasonable to expect them also to spend a great amount of time attempting to pass their skills on to their other siblings. At any rate, their siblings are unlikely to feel as passionate as their gifted brother or sister about expressing themselves in that particular way.

> **FLASHPOINT**
>
> *My younger daughter seems to get very jealous and competitive when my elder daughter does well at school or gets an award. How can I ease this tension?*
>
> Both your children have talents, although it sounds as though the older one has abilities that are recognised particularly often.
>
> What you need to do is to look for things to applaud in your younger daughter's repertoire, so you can lavish genuine praise on her, too.
>
> If you can't currently think of a particular talent, help your younger daughter discover one. When she has nothing specific to do, how does she spend her time? Does she admire a certain celebrity or performer, and if so, why? As soon as you come up with a few ideas, share them with your daughter, and see if together you can come up with a way she could develop that interest.

Age gap between siblings

Another factor affecting school life is the age difference between your children. When there are four or more years between them, any competition is reduced because they're unlikely to pursue the same activities at the same times, or at least to be compared on their performance in those activities simultaneously.

However, when there's a smaller age gap between them, they're liable to be more competitive. Therefore, when two of your children are very close in age, you'll wish to consider very carefully whether they should share the same teachers. When neither feels compelled to live up to the standards of the other, they're less likely to pit themselves against one another. Instead, because they're at similar levels of cognitive and physical development, they can simply both enjoy the same interests and pastimes.

A special case is that of twins or triplets. Many parents agonise about whether it's best, both for their relationship and for the individual needs of each, for them to be in separate classes at school, or to share the same classroom. On the one hand, it could feel traumatic for five-year-olds who've spent almost all their time together up to the school enrolment date, to face two major stresses simultaneously – starting school *and* being separated from one another at the same time. On the other hand, if they are extremely close and they've socialised almost exclusively with one another, they might remain tightly bonded to the exclusion of others and, as a consequence, lose the opportunity to make new friends – and, moreover, to be considered as separate individuals.

Lynn Melby Gordon at California State University recently addressed this issue. She interviewed 131 primary school principals, 54 kindergarten teachers, 201 parents of twins, and 112 twins about whether twins should start school together or in separate classrooms. She conducted these interviews in a state where at that time the school principal was the one who made a unilateral decision about whether or not to assign twins to separate classrooms when they were enrolled at their school. Melby Gordon found that 71% of principals believed that twins should be separated. However, only 49% of kindergarten teachers and 38% of parents agreed. A mere 19% of twins believed it was best to start school in separate classes.

Clearly, whether or not twins should start school in separate classes or as members of the same class is a complicated issue, and no one decision will be the right one for all twins. To make the right decision for your family, talk to the school – the head teacher and the relevant teachers – as well as to your children. Revisit the issue when the children start secondary school, and at this point give a lot of weight to their input, because that's the best way to raise their self-esteem. Involving them in making the decision will also encourage them to feel they can be open and honest with you as well as with one another.

What parents can do ensure a happy school life

Michael Rutter, professor emeritus in child psychology at the University of London, has estimated that children attend school for an average of 15,000 hours. That is a large proportion of their childhood, so it's very important that they're given the best opportunities to thrive while they're at school, and to form positive relationships.

Once your children start school, you'll also wish to consider how best to encourage them to deepen and strengthen the bonds between them, particularly because from now on, they're likely to spend much less time together. If they're close in age and/or highly competitive, it's important that teachers avoid comparing one to the other, which may mean requesting that they're taught by different teachers. Conversely, if one child enjoys nurturing another and the other enjoys this contact, their relationship is likely to become stronger if they pursue similar paths at school – if they have the same teachers and/or if they study some of the same subjects.

Summary

Remember, as your children mature, you'll want to involve them more in making decisions about all the issues that involve them, schooling being just one of them. Remember, too, that although it's never helpful to force siblings to spend time together, keep in mind when you're considering the many aspects of their education that the more time they do spend together (cooperatively, hopefully!), the more memories they'll have to share later on. Siblings who have faced and overcome challenges together will have lots more reminiscing to do when, as adults living independent lives of their own, they get together to remember their childhood.

12

Putting a stop to bullying

When we looked at what to do when your children argue (Part 2, Chapter 8), I encouraged you to let your children sort out their differences themselves whenever it's safe for them to do so. However, there is one exception, and that's when one of your children is bullying another. If this sort of behaviour is repeated, it can all too easily become a habit. This will set up enormous problems both for the bully and for their victim, and it can damage the relationship between them. It's important, therefore, to be able to spot bullying behaviour as soon as it occurs, and to know how to intervene.

If you have a family of three or more you may also recognise that some siblings 'gang up' and work as a team, to the detriment of the other or others. While you want to encourage your children to form close bonds, it's heartbreaking to see one child suffering because of this, however minor it might appear.

Bullying or teasing?

Bullying is the use of force, threat or coercion in order to frighten and dominate another person. The bully intends to cause distress and to prove their dominance over the other person. It can be physical – hitting or pushing, for example; or verbal – taunting or threatening. Nowadays there is also the rising threat of cyberbullying – threatening, humiliating, taunting or harassing other people via electronic communication. Social exclusion – preventing someone joining in with others – is also a form of bullying.

There's a fine line between teasing and bullying. Teasing is provocative, and it's intended to get a reaction from the other person. However, teasing is playful behaviour. It's not *intended* to distress or cause harm. When teasing is no longer playful and becomes hurtful, unkind or unwelcome, it is bullying.

It can be extremely difficult to unpick the difference between teasing and bullying. You need to be aware of the intention of the person who's doing the teasing, but also the interpretation by the person who's being teased. Both intent and interpretation must be benign; otherwise, we're talking about bullying rather than teasing.

Who's likely to become a bully, and why?

Unfortunately, there are no clear-cut characteristics that allow us to identify either a bully or a potential bully, although clinical experience offers some clues.

Bullies are quite often impulsive, and they can find it more difficult than others to think about how others are feeling. There are, however, no obvious physical characteristics that can help us identify bullies – they needn't, for example, be older or bigger than the person they decide to bully. If a child sees someone they admire or someone they consider to be a role model bullying others, and if they conclude that this sort of behaviour seems to 'work', they're more liable to behave in a similar manner, and unfortunately, if left unchecked, this behaviour may continue well into adulthood.

There's a poignant example of this in *The King's Speech,* the film about how George VI overcame his stutter to deliver one of the most important speeches at the end of World War II. Rather than helping him to overcome his tendency to stutter when nervous, his father would become angry and shout at him, only making his stutter worse. In a scene later in the film, his older brother Edward, indignant when his younger sibling confronts him about his relationship with Wallis Simpson, responds by mocking his speech impediment. This bullying temporarily makes his stutter worse and causes him to withdraw his advice because he feels so ashamed of his inability to communicate easily. Sadly, the bullying behaviour had its intended effect.

Bullies invariably feel frustrated or aggrieved in some way, often because they've been bullied themselves, or, as in Edward's case, because he knew his brother was right to admonish him for his irresponsible behaviour, about which he did not want to be challenged.

On the other hand, bullies may feel overlooked or left out by those they consider to be important. They may be jealous because they think that another person is receiving preferential treatment. Or they may simply feel unable to achieve what they want to achieve or to cope adequately in situations where others seem to have little difficulty. Frustrated, feeling helpless and unable to gain attention or praise, they lash out. Their victim may be directly related to their frustration, for example the little sister they feel is their parents' 'favourite'. Or their victim may simply be the person who was nearby when they were feeling most frustrated.

Who's most likely to be bullied, and why?

Most of the time, a bully will choose an individual who doesn't appear particularly self-confident, someone who makes them feel jealous, or someone whom they know is not generally assertive and who may lack good coping strategies when confronted.

Sadly, individuals who are bullied may conclude that the bullying is somehow their own fault, or they may have been told by the bully that there will be dire consequences if they tell anyone. As a result, a bullied child may not ask for help. Therefore, if you're worried that one of your children is being bullied, you need to know how to recognise the signs. These vary widely, but the most common signs are: an increase in fidgeting, skin picking or other nervous habits; an avoidance of eye contact; a lack of appetite; an ongoing sleep disturbance (usually waking in the night repeatedly, often as the result of bad dreams); a refusal to join in social activities; and a repeated avoidance of specific situations or specific social interactions – presumably because the child associates these with the incidents of bullying.

What can parents do to help?

There are a number of excellent charities and other organisations that offer clear and specific advice if you suspect that one of your children is being bullied. You can find a list of them on page 229. This will give you background information about bullying generally, wherever it may occur.

However, we're concerned here with something more specific – bullying between siblings. You will of course wish to put an end to the bullying behaviour as soon as possible, just as you would under any circumstances in which you suspect that your child is bullying or being bullied. Here, however, we're not talking about classmates or even relative strangers. Here, a lifelong relationship is being challenged. Your second aim, therefore, is to help your children repair any damage to their relationship that resulted from the bullying, so they can return to building a strong and positive bond.

Take a long hard look at what's going on right now in your family, and in particular how you and your partner are treating each other and your children.

Ask yourself whether you can feel certain that you're treating your children as fairly as possible. Could it be that you or your partner is inadvertently giving more attention to one of your children? Could it be that you've overlooked the bullying child is some way? One good way to test this possibility is to start observing your reactions to the two children in question. The next time the children you're worried about challenge one another or appear to be arguing, take note of what you do or say – perhaps even write it down afterwards.

If your immediate reaction is to feel angry with one child, while at the same time to feel sorry for the other – *without first examining the validity of the claims of each child* – you'll need to stand back and re-evaluate your assumptions about these two. Both children deserve your concern and neither deserves your anger, because both are hurting. That doesn't mean you should allow this interaction to continue, of course. It simply demonstrates that there may be some truth in the bully's belief that they're being overlooked in preference to the child they're bullying.

Second, think very carefully about how you interact with your partner and with other adults generally. Do you treat others with respect even when you disagree with them? When you argue, do you stick calmly to the issues, or do you become critical of the other person as a whole? Do you threaten your children with punishment if they misbehave, rather than rewarding them with praise when they stick to house rules? Remember, what you *do* counts for far more than anything you tell your children. If you or your partner is exhibiting bullying behaviour, or if you are using threats or coercion to dominate others, you're suggesting by your actions that it's okay to be a bully. Resolve instead to respect different opinions – even if you don't agree with them – and to show by example that the way to resolve differences is by maintaining a mature, thoughtful and responsible approach.

Third – and this is tricky – are you absolutely certain that you know the difference between teasing and bullying? If you tease someone (and consider carefully whether it's really a good idea to tease that person at all) are you quick to apologise sincerely if you inadvertently hurt their feelings? Again, the way you behave counts for far more than anything you might say to your children about what constitutes appropriate behaviour.

How to deal with incidents of bullying

If you suspect that one of your children is being bullied, look out for direct evidence. If instead you feel you must deal with an incident that you've only been *told* about – perhaps because the severity worries you – that's okay, although you have to remain more open-minded because you can't know for sure what actually happened.

As soon as you have a specific incident to discuss, take the two children aside for a talk. Some experts suggest that you speak to each child separately, but I think the presence of both encourages more truth-telling, and with you present, helps the child who's been bullied to feel less frightened.

Start, as always, by asking both of them to take 20 calming breaths (see page 104). Then open with a clear intention: tell them you love them both, but that you're unhappy about their recent behaviour. Your intention is not to punish or to blame, but instead to help them solve whatever the problem is between them. Avoid labels. For example, instead of, 'You shouldn't be such a bully,' you could say, 'Members of this family never pinch other people.' Refer to the specific incident, and ask each child to describe what they believe happened. While each of them has their say, the other is not allowed to interrupt. Ask, too, how each child felt at the time and why they did what they did. Then turn things around and ask each child to try to explain how they think the other child felt. If you must interrupt because there are definite misunderstandings, try to ask questions rather than to correct the child who's speaking. Your aim is not to 'take over', but rather to encourage them to correct themselves.

Now ask each of them to suggest at least one other way they might handle this 'misunderstanding' next time. Could John offer Grace a different toy, perhaps? Is there somewhere John could play where Grace couldn't snatch his toys? Offer suggestions yourself if neither is forthcoming, but don't force your views. Use them only as a starting point. The aim is to get the children to come up with solutions they feel are their own. To achieve this, you may have to be patient and to settle for less than perfect – as long, of course, as the solution is cooperative rather than power-based.

Finish by praising both children genuinely, and help them – there and then – to make any changes they've decided to make so that they can get on better. If your partner wasn't with you during this encounter, it will add importance to the occasion if you tell them all about what happened in front of the children, emphasising each child's efforts and kindness towards the other.

You'll now have to be more watchful for a time, especially if you think that this sort of behaviour has been going on for a while. It takes about three to four weeks to break a habit, so be patient. Whenever you notice another bullying incident, respond to it in the way I've just described, and do so as soon as possible. The sooner you react, the fresher will be the memory of the incident, so the more likely it is that each child will remember their feelings.

Finally, find as many opportunities as you can to ask the two of them to do something that requires them to cooperate. For example, you might ask them to tidy up their play area together. Keep an eye on them. Praise every example of cooperative behaviour lavishly, pointing out specifically why you're so pleased. For example, you might say, 'John, what a helpful child you were! You picked up your toys, but you also helped Grace tidy hers away so you could both finish at the same time.'

Summary

Bullying is a common and very distressing problem. The best way to deal with it is to avoid blame or reprimand, but instead to use bullying incidents to teach your children the importance of thinking before acting, and of always trying to consider what a situation looks like from the other person's point of view.

13

Over-responsibility

There is one problem regarding sibling relationships that you don't hear much about. There are two reasons for this. First, when your children are young, it's generally not seen as a problem. Second, almost all the advice given to parents about how best to raise their children focuses only on the time when the children are growing up. There's little, if anything, that looks ahead to adulthood and suggests what parents can do to ensure that their children will continue to have positive, close relationships once they've grown up and established families of their own.

Over-responsibility is something that can have a very detrimental effect on an individual as well as on their relationships with their siblings in adulthood. The reason that over-responsibility can so easily become established during childhood is that during the early years, it appears benign – in fact, at times, it's even seen as an asset. This happens most often in families where the parents feel stretched to their limits with the demands of childcare, work and other obligations. Without thinking, they may start to encourage one of their children to take on more and more caring responsibilities, without at the same time making sure that child is also rewarded for pursuing things they love to do for themselves. As a result, that child will develop some unhelpful and unhealthy beliefs and behaviours about what is an 'appropriate' level of responsibility, both with regard to their siblings and towards other people generally. Furthermore, their self-esteem will be fragile, because their sense of worth will depend entirely on whether they're caring for others rather than for themselves.

What is over-responsibility?

To understand the consequences of over-responsibility, we need to start with a definition. Over-responsibility is best described as 'feeling the need to be accountable not only for your own actions and decisions, but also for those of other people, whether they ask for help or not'. This is not the same as a desire to help – that's pure generosity, and the aim of it is to empower the person or cause we're addressing. Over-responsibility is different: the overly responsible person assumes that the other person is incapable of accomplishing whatever they're struggling to do without their input, and, furthermore, that they're the only person who can give that help properly. Overly responsible individuals derive their sense of self-worth from feeling they are needed. Their definition of self-worth may be summed up like this: 'I'm only any good if I'm helping.'

I expect you may have heard about over-responsibility when it applies to children whose parents are themselves rendered incapable in some way, perhaps through drug or alcohol dependency or severe depression. But we seldom hear about children who are asked to assume too much responsibility for the care of their siblings even though their parents are not physically or mentally incapacitated. Nonetheless, it does happen. Over-responsibility does not usually become a habit if a child is only occasionally overburdened. However, if they're asked to help to the limit of their capabilities (or beyond those capabilities), if they're asked to do so regularly and often, if they're rarely encouraged or praised for doing things that express their own individuality, and if their own need to be cared for and valued simply for 'being', as opposed to 'doing', is continually overlooked, they'll become driven by a sense of over-responsibility.

The consequences for all the children in the family are not good. The over-burdened child is filled with ambivalence. On the one hand, they're proud to be considered so needed and so capable. At the same time, however, they feel trapped and burdened by the needs of others, and helpless when things don't go to plan. Their need to control situations that are often beyond their capabilities may lead to chronic anxiety and fatigue. Eventually, when they're in the work environment, they will be more prone than others to burnout. When they're older, they may find that their constant need to offer advice – whether asked for or not – makes them unpopular. Their inability to delegate because they don't feel able to trust others to do things exactly their way means that they'll never be truly successful.

The cared-for children don't fare well, either. If they're fairly passive and cooperative by nature, they'll accept the help offered without resistance. As a result, however, they'll remain dependent and they're unlikely to mature and develop independent living skills as quickly as they might. Because of this dependence and reliance on the overly responsible sibling, they'll miss out on the wonderful satisfaction of having achieved something through their own efforts. If the child being cared for is more strong-willed, their sibling's solicitous, over-attentive ministrations will create resentment, and make them avoid the 'helpful' sibling rather than enjoy their companionship.

When the children are young and they really do still need to be looked after, assigning one child to fulfil that role may appear to work well, and may feel like a relief for you. The younger ones are safe (although they're not learning to become more independent), the 'responsible' child glows with their parents' praise for their efforts, and some of the burden of care is lifted from your own shoulders. However, when the over-burdened child becomes an adolescent and wants increasingly to spend time with their friends, they'll begin to resent this burden of care. This may also be the time when cared-for siblings start to want to 'do it myself'. The result? Growing resentment and negative feelings between your children.

Overly responsible teenagers may experience particular difficulties during adolescence. Their need to control and to impose their way of doing things on everyone else will alienate them, leaving them feeling isolated from their peers and resented by their siblings. One good coping reaction – although not necessarily the best reason for choosing a life direction – is to pursue a career in the caring professions. Here, an overly responsible individual will find a more 'acceptable' outlet for their desire to help others. Alas, however, they're more likely than their colleagues to feel over-burdened and resentful.

If this pattern of interaction between siblings is never addressed, yet another problem may arise in mid-life. By this time, their parents may need some help themselves, and because of habit, they'll appeal first to the overly responsible sibling. If that individual hasn't let go of their need to control others, and if the siblings haven't repaired their relationships, then the overly responsible sibling may find that they're shouldering the entire burden of caring for increasingly frail parents. What a pity this is! Caring for our parents, although it can be exhausting and at times very distressing, is one of the best ways for adult siblings to come together again and re-affirm their lifelong bond. It's also a time for sharing memories, for 'completing' the task of becoming fully independent. This is best done with everyone working together. That's only possible if each of the 'children' feels equally responsible for their parents' care, and only if they care for and support one another throughout this process. The care each gives may not be 'equal' in terms of time or cost, but each must be seen to contribute fairly by the others.

What you can do to encourage closeness and equality among your children

The most valuable gift a parent can give to their children is unconditional love. This means accepting and loving each one for their unique qualities. This is the best way not only to raise happy, self-confident children, but also to raise children who grow up enjoying the company of their siblings rather than feeling hostile towards them, competing against them for your attention.

Of course, that's not the only thing you need to do. It's also important to be a good role model, to set and maintain clear house rules, to make sure that your children develop good social skills and learn to be empathetic, and to encourage everyone to show warmth and mutual respect for one another.

In practical terms, how do parents go about achieving this?

Delegate tasks and responsibilities equally and appropriately

It's good for children to develop a sense of responsibility, to understand that living with others is most harmonious when everyone contributes to the general good. They'll also feel great pride in their accomplishments. However, the responsibilities you give them must not be excessive, and should be in keeping with each child's level of development. So, for example, a five-year-old can be expected to make their own bed, to put their dirty clothes in the laundry basket, and to help clear dishes after a meal. A ten-year-old, on the other hand, is capable of much more. For example, they can be asked to help you prepare a meal, or to feed the family pet. A teenager could plan and cook a family meal entirely on their own, or help a younger sibling with their homework – as long as they have plenty of time left to do their own homework. You'll need to reconsider what makes for a fair contribution from each child on a regular basis, so you reflect each child's growing independence. The key is that the distribution of responsibility is fair, not excessive, appropriately challenging, and that it leaves each child with adequate time to pursue their own interests and friendships as well.

Assign your children tasks that are best done together as a team

You will know from Chapter 7 how valuable teamwork is when it comes to strengthening the bonds between your children. Their experiences will also create fond memories for them to share when they're older – even, or perhaps especially, when things don't go according to plan. So, for example, rather than asking one child to feed the hamster, explain to them all that the hamster needs to be fed, to be given clean water, and to have its cage cleaned out once a day, and that they must decide who will carry out each of those jobs, preferably at similar times.

Praise each child for their care of siblings and their contribution to the household, but equally for their own efforts at self-expression

Note that I am asking you to praise them for their *efforts* at self-expression. Accomplishments are worthy of praise, too, of course, but accomplishments depend not only on effort, but also on factors that are outside an individual's control. Therefore, when you praise effort, you target the one aspect of achievement that your child will always be able to control. This encourages them to take on new challenges and to pursue their dreams, however difficult it may seem to achieve those dreams. When your children feel free to be themselves they'll be happier. When they know they'll be praised just for trying hard, never mind whether they win or lose, they'll dare to take on difficult but potentially rewarding challenges. Praising effort and uniqueness is the counter-balance to taking communal responsibility. It means that each of your children has the best chance of becoming an independent and self-assured adult, while at the same time developing their unique personality.

Be a good role model: take good care of and enjoy yourself

If you allow yourself to be swamped with responsibilities, and if you neglect your own health and happiness in a ceaseless effort to sort out everyone and everything else, your children are unlikely to look forward to growing up! You'll also encourage them to become overly responsible.

You are the most powerful role model for your children, and they're likely to follow in your footsteps. Therefore, it's your duty not only to show empathy and responsibility, but also to model the importance of valuing yourself rather than struggling, unhappy and tired, to always 'be there' for everyone else.

Therefore, take good care of your health, both physical and mental. Decide for yourself what your priorities are, and learn to say 'no' to unnecessary obligations in a way that makes it clear that you mean it. When you behave in this way, your children will understand how to maintain a balance between doing for others and taking care of themselves – and they'll thank you for it.

Summary

Over-responsibility is a subtle problem, because during childhood, it may seem innocuous. To prevent your children developing this tendency, make sure that when you ask them to take responsibility, it's something well within their capabilities, and also that the obligation doesn't become so dominant that they must neglect their own interests and enthusiasms – and the latter deserve as much praise from you as when they take responsibility. Make sure, too, that any responsibilities you ask of one child doesn't put a strain on their relationship with their siblings. Finally, as your children's most important role model, make sure that you maintain a balance between caring for others and taking good care of yourself.

14

When an adult child returns to live at home

The number of step-families is on the rise, but the rate of increase is nothing compared to the increase in the number of adult children returning to the family home to live for a time. Scarcity of jobs, financial uncertainty, and the incredibly high cost of renting or buying a property mean that many young people, even when they try to be careful, are running into debt and/or losing their jobs. Coming back home to live for a time may be the only realistic option, and it's often the norm when a child finishes their university course. Many parents feel surprised and stressed by this sudden addition to the household, and many young people suffer a blow to their self-esteem, feeling that they've 'failed' in some way.

Nonetheless, this period at home can be a very positive experience if it's handled sensitively and pragmatically. Dealing with the 'returner', as I shall refer to this (now grown-up) child, presents a number of challenges. If you have younger children still living at home, the challenges multiply. At the very least, parents will have to deal with the stress this will impose on sibling relationships at home, as everyone readjusts to the returner.

As is the case with regard to the introduction of step-siblings, there is almost no good academic research on returners. This is such a recent phenomenon that there's simply been no time to gather meaningful data. Therefore, once again I will be relying on clinical experience, on the ways in which patients and returners in my clinics have identified and dealt with the issues that arise when a returner moves back into the family home.

The size of the phenomenon

We are not talking here about small numbers or gradual trends. The Office for National Statistics (ONS) claims that nearly half of the UK's 20- to 24-year-olds were living at home with their parents in 2015. The figures are highest in Northern Ireland, with the West Midlands, Northwest England, East England and Wales not far behind. The areas where the figures are lowest are London and Yorkshire and the Humber, followed by East Midlands and Southwest England. Taken as a whole, however, the rate of increase has been incredibly rapid: the ONS claims that there's been a 42% rise in 20–24-year-olds living at home since 2008.

The different perspectives of family members

Parents

Parents are often initially surprised – although increasingly less so – when their adult son or daughter asks to move back in. This is often followed by irritation and confusion: 'I had everything figured out and sorted. Now I have to think again!'

The reaction that most often comes next is guilt. Parents assume they must have misjudged their child's circumstances, and, very often, that they did something wrong at some point in their upbringing. This is almost always nonsense, of course. This new trend has far more to do with economics than with childcare practices. At any rate, this tendency to feel guilty is not helpful, because it often means that parents become over-solicitous towards their returner, treating them again as a child. This only exacerbates any feelings of failure that the returner may have.

The returner

Returners may come straight from university, and if so, the move home is less surprising – just a break before getting a job and renting a flat. More often than not, however, the sojourn at home becomes lengthier than expected, and this can lead to feelings of failure, a heightened loss of direction and fear that they are not doing what they're 'supposed' to do.

Returners who didn't go to university, or who have made a life for themselves after completing their studies, almost always contact parents only as a last resort. It usually happens after they've tried a number of ways to maintain their independence, and it has usually come about after some personal crisis such as an unexpected job loss or the breakup of a relationship. Sometimes the landlord in the flat they're renting decides to sell the property and the tenants find it difficult to find another comparable place to rent. Sometimes – although this is fairly rare – the returner has been careless and has racked up unsustainable debts.

Because of their circumstances, these returners almost always feel that they've failed in some way, even when what happened wasn't their fault. They, like their parents, also feel guilty for not foreseeing what was about to happen, even though it probably wouldn't have been possible. If they're a firstborn, they'll feel particularly sensitive about being perceived as a failure, because they were likely to have been considered a high achiever at home and at school. They also worry about feeling restricted, about the possibility of being treated as a child again if they return to live with their parents. They may also wish to avoid their younger siblings because they feel ashamed that they've not coped with independent living.

The other children in the family

If there are younger children still at home, they will have adjusted to a new pecking order when the older child moved out. In particular, the next child down becomes, in many senses, the responsible eldest. That child will be most worried about their elder sibling returning home, fearing that they'll lose their status among the remaining siblings and their parents. They may withdraw, and become sullen or angry. Their relationship with their older sibling, once based on admiration, may become laced with antagonism and resentment.

Any other younger siblings will feel less directly threatened, although they may wonder if they'll be displaced and have to move to a smaller or different bedroom. If their parents seem excessively worried about the returner, all the other siblings will feel threatened and uncomfortable, suddenly less important in their parents' estimation. They may also worry that when they leave home, they, too, may find it impossible to cope.

How parents can help

It's important that you approach this situation with several aims in mind, rather than just the one intention of helping the returner.

Of course, it will be absolutely vital to help the returner restore their sense of self-confidence. You need to help them do so not only for their own sake, however. Your younger children will benefit as well. They'll feel relieved, because they can see now that it's possible to stand up again and return to a fully independent existence, even after a stumble.

When the returner begins to feel more optimistic and confident, they'll become a positive role model for the younger ones once more. Furthermore, the older, well-established and more positive feelings your children all have for one another will resurface once the returner stops feeling guilty and inadequate, and once the younger ones realise that the returner has no desire to remain at home and resume their former position as the eldest of the 'children'.

As the returner gradually regains their self-confidence – and this can take some months – your second aim is to make it clear to your other children that they are just as important to you as ever, and that things will not change greatly at home. If they don't feel threatened by the returner or diminished in your eyes, the chance that sibling bonds will deteriorate is negligible.

Here, then, are some specific guidelines.

Treat the situation as temporary

It's important that you behave as if you fully expect your returner to regain a positive attitude and to return to independent living as soon as possible.

Regard the returner as an adult

Your returner is not a large child, but an adult who needs time to rethink their direction. Encourage them to shop for themselves, to prepare their own meals, and to keep their room and possessions sorted themselves. Do *not* continually offer to help. Your confidence in them will help the returner enormously; if you appear certain that they'll be back on their own feet again soon, it will be so much easier for them to believe that as well.

Reduce the sense of threat to younger siblings

It's important for all your children to see you behaving as if you fully expect your returner to regain a positive attitude and to return to independent living. The younger ones will also relax if you continue to treat them just as you did before the returner came home.

Set clear terms and conditions

Draw up a specific contract with the returner, including a clear time limit for staying at home. This will help them focus on finding a job, new accommodation, repaying their debts, and whatever else contributed to their need to return home. Involve them fully in setting the parameters.

A business arrangement, not a rescue operation

Make sure the returner pays rent. Decide the rate together, an amount that everyone feels is reasonable. Remember, it's not the amount that matters, but rather that paying rent connotes adult status. This, more than anything else, will remind them that they're only staying temporarily.

When my own daughter returned home at 24, for example, we worked out what she could reasonably earn and what her proportion of household expenses (apart from food, which she bought herself) she should pay. Initially, her earnings and her proportion of costs couldn't match, so she paid very little rent. However, as time went by and she paid off her debts and increased her earnings with a better job, she was able to pay her proper share. Her self-confidence rose further as a result.

Stay out of the returner's room

Treat them just as you would a stranger who is lodging with you. Their space is their own. This will help them feel more mature.

Respect each other's needs and schedules

Give the returner their own set of keys. Expect them to come and go as they please, but at the same time, make it clear that they in turn must respect everyone else's schedules and their need for quiet at certain times.

Minimise any other changes at home

Try to avoid making any changes whatsoever in your other children's living arrangements and schedules. Do *not*, for example, ask anyone to 'give up their room' for the returner. If bathroom space is limited, you may have to mark out different places for everyone to keep their shampoo and other toiletries. (It would help greatly to avoid any tension if you could install a basin in the returner's room.)

Summary

Once your returner begins to see their way ahead again, and the younger ones feel reassured that their status hasn't changed in their parents' estimation, you'll notice that they'll start bantering with one another just as they used to, and that they will begin to enjoy spending some time together again.

Try not to step in and orchestrate these occasions. As long as everyone seems happy, allow them to re-establish their relationships with one another in their own way. You'll probably notice, by the way, that those relationships are now even stronger and more positive than they were before the returner left home originally.

15

Helping maintain sibling bonds in adulthood

Throughout this book, we've focused primarily on your children's relationships with other family members while they're young and still living with you. However, the relationships with you and with their siblings will endure beyond their childhood years, and the sibling relationships in particular will help form the bedrock of their stability later in life. The relationships with their siblings are likely to be the longest-lasting relationships they'll ever have.

Sibling relationships go through a 'life cycle', a natural ebb and flow, as levels of intimacy wane and are then revitalised. This is determined by your children's ages, their challenges at the time, and the stage of life they're going through at any given time.

The life cycle of sibling bonds

When your children are young, their relationships with their siblings will be intense, a mixture of jealousy, rivalry, warmth, loyalty and mutual support. This is the time when the foundations of their relationships with their brothers and sisters – and, therefore, with peers throughout their lives – will be laid down. The way you deal with each of your children and the way you handle their interactions will be the critical factor that determines how well they'll relate to one another, as well as to their friends, their partners and their colleagues when they're adults.

During their teenage years, your children will appear to be less concerned with and less reliant on one another. If you've helped them develop trusting, cooperative and supportive bonds instead of encouraging them to compete with one another, then whenever they're in crisis – when a partner rejects them, or when they fail to achieve a cherished goal, for example – they're likely to turn to their siblings for support, and for confirmation that they're still lovable. But other than that, teenagers are far more focused on their peer relationships than they are on their relationships with the members of their family.

Therefore, there's no need to worry if your teenagers seem to 'cool off' and become distant towards one another during adolescence. This is only temporary. It's important, however, to make sure that everyone still gets together regularly, for example for a meal a couple of times a week. On those occasions, encourage the atmosphere of open acceptance that, hopefully, you will already have established long ago. That way, communication lines will stay open in the family, and teenagers will be reminded that you and their siblings are there if ever they need you. But other than that, don't worry if they seem distant from the rest of you, or if they seem moody or uninterested in the rest of the family. They're not uninterested – not really. They're simply focused elsewhere, on establishing their place within their peer group.

When your children reach adulthood, the apparent distance between them may continue during their 20s and 30s. Again, don't worry. They're finding their own direction in life, establishing their independence and perhaps starting a family of their own.

However, the efforts you made when your children were young – offering them opportunities to work together, helping them resolve conflicts constructively, respectfully and amicably, and establishing family traditions – will have paid off. Helgola Ross and Joel Milgram at the University of Cincinnati in Ohio interviewed 75 adults of all ages (from 22 to 93) across a wide range of educational and family backgrounds. They concluded that the factors most strongly associated with closeness between adult siblings were their geographical proximity – how close they lived to one another; the number of positive memories they shared; whether they met up for reunions regularly; and, most important of all, the quality of the relationships they forged during childhood.

You're unlikely to have any say about where they settle as adults, of course. But you are central in establishing the quality of their relationships in childhood and in making sure they have plenty of adventures together and traditions to remember and share again in later life.

Sibling relationships become increasingly important as we grow older. Victor Cicirelli, Professor of Psychology at Purdue University in Indiana, has spent much of his career studying sibling relationships in adulthood and old age. He has found that almost all siblings stay in contact with one another throughout the whole of their lives, particularly when the interactions they established early in life were warm and positive. Sisters tend to maintain contact with one another most frequently, brother and sister pairs less so, and brother–brother pairs least of all. Nonetheless, when interviewed, 68% of adults, both male and female, said that they still felt 'close or extremely close' to their siblings throughout middle age.

By the time we reach old age, our relationships with our siblings assume a truly central focus in our lives, becoming perhaps an even greater source of comfort and security to us than when we were children and we had our parents to rely on for support as well. Cicirelli found that 83% of adults in their 60s and beyond felt 'close or extremely close' to their siblings. When a sibling dies during this period, surviving siblings speak of a sense of 'incompleteness' and a loss of identity, so profound is the loss. They also said that they felt closer to their living siblings as a result.

Cicirelli found that another reason why older adults value their relationships with their siblings is because they know that they can always rely on their brothers and sisters to help them if they need it. He and other researchers have found that this willingness to be on 'stand by' is strongly associated with a sense of wellbeing in old age – even though in fact, he notes that older siblings rarely do call on one another for tangible help. It's the knowledge that someone is always there and willing, someone who knows us well, rather than any material assistance that comforts us during this time in our lives.

Sibling relationships during adolescence and adulthood

Communication is the key

Throughout the years when your children are living at home, keep communication lines open. It's never too early to start. Make sure, for example, that you share several meals together every week. On those occasions, and whenever else the opportunity arises, ensure that everyone listens respectfully and non-judgementally to the others.

Show them good problem-solving and social skills

From the time they can talk, help them resolve interpersonal conflicts constructively, and praise them when they do so. (See Part 2.)

Establish family traditions

For example, decide how you want to spend Christmas, or how you'll celebrate each child's birthday. Keep these traditions going for as long as possible, even when they're adults. Once they've moved away, invite their partners and your grandchildren as well, to make those times together even more enjoyable and memorable for everyone.

Arrange an annual get-together

If you can afford to do it, it would be wonderful for your children – and, later on, for your grandchildren – if you could rent a large cottage for a week, perhaps the same week every year. Invite all the children and, later on, include their families as well for an annual reunion.

Fill their childhood with cooperative adventures

Throughout their lives, but particularly during childhood, make sure your children have lots of memorable experiences together. Build in lots of cooperative ventures – making meals together, spending a day by the seaside, caring collectively for a family pet. Not only will everyone enjoy these activities at the time, but they'll be able to relive their shared adventures over and over again, whenever they get together to re-affirm the relationships that have comforted them, and will continue to comfort them, throughout the whole of their lives.

Summary

Your children's relationships with each other are generally the longest-lasting relationships they'll ever have. Start laying the foundations now for those relationships to be strong, positive and affirming. Establish traditions, teach them how to resolve conflicts constructively, and above all, keep communication lines open.

Part 4

Specific challenges

16

Multiple births

What happens to sibling relations when there is no age gap? What is the relationship likely to be between twins, triplets or more born at the same time? How true are assumptions that a twin bond is the strongest sibling bond possible, or that twins are more likely to struggle to find their own identity? And what about the relationship between multiple birth children and their other siblings? How can parents ensure that all their children in such families bond as strongly and as positively as possible?

Note: To make things simpler, I will use 'twins' to mean all multiple births throughout this chapter.

Nowadays about 1.6% of pregnant women give birth to more than one child. According to the ONS, in 2015 this represented 11,073 mothers in the UK. Nearly all multiple births (10,901) were twins, 169 were triplets, and three were quadruplets or more. For our purposes, it's very important to note as well that a disproportionate number of these mothers are older – over 45 years of age. This is probably associated with the fact that women who opt for IVF treatment usually do so when they're older, after having tried to conceive a child for some years. On average, one in ten IVF pregnancies results in a multiple birth, whereas for other women the chances of a multiple birth are one in 80. Furthermore, a large proportion – about half – of multiple birth babies are born by Caesarean section.

Both of these factors – being older and possibly having just had major surgery – plus the fact that carrying more than one child makes even greater demands on the mum than carrying only one, means that many mothers who give birth to two or more babies face a daunting physical challenge when trying to recover from the birth and at the same time to give full attention to more than one infant. It certainly sets the scene for strong competition between siblings as they jostle to have their (generally simultaneous) needs met.

Identical or non-identical?

An important aspect of twin births to consider is what proportion are identical and what proportion are non-identical or fraternal. About a third of twins are identical; about half of these are male pairs and about half are female pairs. Another third are boy–girl fraternal twins. The remaining third of twin births are same-sex fraternal pairs, and again about half are male pairs and half are females.

Many people attribute a special status to identical twins and, to a lesser extent, to same-sex fraternal twins. Surely, the thinking goes, if two babies are physically identical, they'll develop a much closer bond than will fraternal twins who, apart from the timing of their birth, are in every other way like any other pair of siblings. Furthermore, many people believe that twins who share the same gender, whether identical or fraternal, will be closer than a brother–sister pair will be. How true, or helpful, are these assumptions?

There's no evidence to show that identical twins and same-sex fraternal twins necessarily bond more closely than male–female twins. True, they share more characteristics. But that is exactly what may cause them to be more rivalrous than to get on easily! The more similar one child is to another, the harder they must work to obtain the one thing they want most of all – to be considered unique and special by their parents. Keep reading for advice on how you can encourage their sense of identity.

The relationship between multiples

Everyone assumes that twins will have a particularly close relationship, having shared the same environment even before birth. We need to balance that shared experience, however, with the knowledge that they'll also need parental care and attention at the same time while they're growing up. With only one set of parents to meet this double demand, although they may be close because of so much shared experience, they'll also be rivalrous because of their need to compete with one another for parental attention. You might think that this will merely serve to increase the strength of their bond – after all, as you learned in Chapter 8, strong bonds are created when individuals experience intense emotions towards one another, whether the emotions are primarily positive and cooperative or more aggressive and competitive.

Nancy Segal, professor of psychology at California State University, Fullerton, and founder of the Twin Studies Center, has studied twins for over 25 years, and was a leading researcher in what's probably the most well-known study of twins, the Minnesota Twin Family Study. This study, begun in 1989 by Thomas Bouchard, has followed, and continues to follow, 1,400 pairs of twins. These include identical and same-sex fraternal twins. Some were raised apart and some together. All were either 11 or 17 years old in 1989. The researchers now have evidence to suggest that on balance, twins are more competitive than cooperative, although identical twins appear to be less competitive than fraternal twins.

The Minnesota study has also highlighted some extraordinary similarities between identical siblings, even when raised apart. One pair of twin males who were raised apart, for example, married women with the same name, gave their dogs the same name, and even chose similar cars. This is but one of several examples. In others, identical twins raised apart chose the same careers, despite growing up in totally different circumstances both financially and academically. However, before we take these similarities too much to heart, it's important to note that journalists in particular – but researchers as well – tend to highlight only the similarities between the pairs of twins they study, while at the same time overlooking their differences. That's not to say that the similarities are not striking. They are. But the emphasis may not always be evenly balanced.

Intelligence as measured by IQ also appears to be far more similar in identical twins than in other sibling pairs, and once again, even when the twins are raised apart. For example, the Minnesota Twin Family Study has found that 85% of identical twins raised together have essentially the same IQ, whereas this is true for only about 60% of fraternal twins raised in the same home.

Bernie Devlin and his colleagues at the Pittsburgh School of Medicine looked into heritability and IQ in even more detail. In 1997 they published a 'meta-analysis' (an overview of the results of a number of similar studies) in the journal *Nature*. In Devlin's study, the team combined the results of 212 studies that looked at IQ in twins. They found that the similarity of IQ of identical twins is substantially greater than that of any other sibling pairs, even when identical twins are raised apart. They concluded, as in the Minnesota study, that 85% of identical twins raised together shared the same IQ. However, a startlingly high 74% of identical twins raised apart also had the same IQ. This is a much closer match than the IQs of non-identical twins, as well as of other sibling pairs. Whereas 45% of siblings raised together had the same IQ, only 24% of those raised apart scored the same. These findings point strongly to a genetic component of IQ. However, Devlin also suggests another possibility; that the reason for the difference between identical twins and other siblings may in part be because identical twins share the same womb environment during the first nine months after conception. He suggests, quite plausibly, that the conditions in the womb during gestation may also profoundly influence IQ scores.

Longitudinal studies are the best way to tease apart the relative contributions of genetics and environment when we consider the differences between identical twins and other sibling pairs. Unfortunately, other than the Minnesota study, there are very few of these. However, Britta Akerman, a professor in Stockholm, has followed 32 twin pairs from birth. In 2003, when the twins were 16, she published some interesting data concerning personality differences. Overall, she found that fraternal twins scored more highly on creativity than did identical twins, but that at the same time boys in boy–girl pairs were more creative than boys in boy–boy pairs. She also found that girls in fraternal pairs were more confident than girls in identical twin pairs. This is a relatively small study, so we must be very careful about generalising any of Akerman's findings. However, what her results suggest is that twins who are more distinct from one another, whether because of their gender or their physical appearance, are more likely to express their uniqueness.

These findings only add force to my overarching advice in this chapter – that the more often you treat each of your twins as an individual, different from the other, the more likely it is that each will feel confident to express their individuality. My belief is that they'll also be happier as a result.

Finally, you may have heard that some twins, particularly identical twins, develop their own 'secret language'. This is known as 'idioglossia' ('same sounds') or 'cryptophasia' ('secret speech'). Perhaps the most intriguing pair who were said to have developed their own language were June and Jennifer Gibbons, known as the 'Silent Twins' in the 1986 BBC docudrama of that name. June and Jennifer were born in Barbados in 1963, and shortly thereafter their father was transferred to an RAF station in Haverfordwest in Wales, where the girls were reportedly bullied because they were the only black children at the school. As young children, they were said to have developed a secret language. On closer inspection, however, this language, like so many 'secret' twin languages, looked more like a mixture of the dialects and expressions the twins had heard as they were growing up, rather than being classifiable as an entirely new language. Although there's still debate about the existence of 'secret' twin communication, most of us now believe that what develops is not a distinct and completely new language, but rather a habitual way of communicating using sounds that contain the fragments of the language or languages to which the children have been exposed.

In summary, it appears that most identical twins grow up to be closer, more cooperative and more alike than fraternal twins. Fraternal same-sexed twins are also likely to be close but, relative to identical twins, more competitive than cooperative. At the same time, the more each twin – whether that child is one of an identical pair or one of a fraternal pair – is regarded as different from the other, the more likely it is that each will develop their individual strengths and grow up feeling less competitive in relation to their twin.

What parents can do

When parenting twins or multiples, there is one piece of advice that overreaches everything: treat them as unique individuals as often as possible. This is the best way to ensure positive relationships within the family and with the outside world. While it's easy to group children together into 'the twins' or even 'the girls/boys', you may be creating more of a reason for them to vie for your time and affections, as they do not feel that you recognise them for who they are individually. In very basic terms, it would work best to ignore the fact that your children are multiples and treat them exactly the same as children in any other sibling relationship.

Recover well

The first and most important rule if you're raising more than one child at the same time is to make your own wellbeing and physical recovery a priority. This is true after any birth, of course, but it's especially important in multiple births, when your body has been particularly challenged.

When you're feeling well, your babies will be calmer and easier to soothe. This is because they easily sense any distress their carer feels. They'll also feel more competitive for your attention if they sense that attention is more limited because you're exhausted. Try never to think of good self-care as 'indulgent'. Think of it instead as vital to your babies' wellbeing.

Furthermore, even if you do feel relatively rested, don't be afraid or embarrassed to ask for help. You and your children will benefit, particularly if you have other children besides the twins. The more often you can be sure that each child receives adequate attention, the less reason each child will have to be jealous of the others, and, therefore, the more you'll be doing to encourage positive relationships between all of them.

Language

From the outset, watch how you refer to your children. When friends stop by, or when they stop you when you're out to admire the new arrivals – and they most definitely will – take care never to refer to them as 'the twins' or 'the triplets'. The sooner and the more often you treat each one as an individual, pointing out proudly the unique qualities of each, the more likely it is that each will grow up confident, independent, and fond of their sibling instead of aggressively anxious to establish the differences between themselves and the other. I'm sure it's obvious, too, that it would be unwise to dress them alike, give them identical hairstyles, or saddle them with indistinguishable or rhyming names. Avoid labelling them as well – she's 'the sleepy one'; he's 'the anxious one' – as this is an indirect way of comparing them, thus setting up competition or feelings of rivalry and, often, of inferiority on the part of one of them, particularly later on.

Sleeping

Once they're beyond the infant stage (if not even before), you'll want to start thinking about longer-term sleeping arrangements. Try to regard this issue just as you would when you're dealing with any other group of siblings. Every one of us needs our own space, somewhere we can truly call our own. Separate bedrooms for those who would like to have that arrangement, if you have that sort of space, is brilliant. However, any 'own space' is good, no matter how small the area. I once worked with a family who had only one bedroom available for all four of their children. They stretched old sheets across wire clothes dryers to create screens, so they could separate the children. Each was given a bedside light, and even in these straitened conditions a personal space was thus created for each child.

Life with twins

Once they start school, parents of twins face one of their most difficult decisions. Should the children share the same classroom, or would it be better to separate them, to put them into separate classes with different teachers? The issue of same or separate classrooms, different teachers, or even of different schools, is discussed in detail in Chapter 11.

Another question that will inevitably arise is how to arrange birthday parties. When your twins are young, it's fine to hold a joint party, and it's probably the only realistic thing you can manage. On the other hand, when they're older – adolescents, and perhaps even a bit before – separate parties, if you can make that possible, will allow each to feel special, to express their developing individuality, and to invite their own particular friends.

Finally, there is the question of friendships. You'll need to be on the lookout, even more diligently than you would be with other sibling groups, for the different friendships that each child is forming. Try to encourage those friendships, because this is another way to enhance the individuality of each twin. Be prepared, however, for some surprisingly powerful feelings of jealousy when one twin claims to have found a 'best friend'. Their sibling may feel hurt and left out, or may jealously try to 'steal' this new friend's affections. Try to see this as a third person 'intruding' on a previously almost exclusive, very special relationship. The best way to deal with the situation – besides recognising that the intensely rivalrous feelings are unlikely to last – is to find ways to help the one who is excluded from the new relationship to find a best friend of their own.

Being a sibling of a set of multiples

This is one of the most difficult, as well as one of the most overlooked, parenting challenges. Twins can always turn to one another for comfort if they feel alone or overlooked. No such compensation exists for their siblings. This is a particular problem if you have a child who's older than your twins, and it's by finding ways to address this issue head on at the start that you'll have most success. Besides teaching them by your example to listen to each other respectfully, create opportunities for each twin to spend some enjoyable exclusive time with one other sibling (other than their twin). Do this as often as possible, throughout their childhood and into early adolescence, until they're obviously ready to spend the majority of their time out and about with friends. By this time, however, they will have established strong and positive bonds across their sibling group, something they'll thank you for in early adulthood and beyond.

When twins are born

When twins or multiples are born, there's no doubt that your other children will feel the loss of attention keenly – not just from over-stretched parents, but also from admiring visitors and relatives.

Consider in particular a first-born child. They will have had the unique experience of enjoying the exclusive attention of all main carers. Suddenly, they lose this exclusivity and attention. Now they've lost status to two new babies, so in effect they've lost all chances of being regarded as 'special' by casual observers. To make things even more painful for the older child, he or she also feels excluded from the close bond between the twins. This comes across as an overwhelming rejection, and it can create powerful feelings of jealousy. The effects can be so overwhelming that the older child may become withdrawn or even depressed – a rare event for young children. Alternatively, the older child may regress, and/or become hugely demonstrative and demanding.

The intensity of such feelings is less for siblings born after twins, because they come into the world accepting that parental attention must be shared. Nonetheless they, too, are deprived of the admiring attention of outsiders that the twins will enjoy.

It will be incredibly difficult for you to get this one right, to create a situation that encourages the development of high self-esteem in your twins as well as in the other siblings in the family. You may have to be quite creative in seeking out ways to find time to give some regular one-to-one attention to the siblings who are not twins.

Get some extra regular help. Ask relatives or friends, or hire a professional if you can afford it. It's money well spent. Even a couple of hours a week could make a tremendous difference.

It's preferable to ask the helper to look after the twins, while you give some time to the other child or children. An outsider is likely to enjoy the novelty of caring for twins. Meanwhile, you can spend some time with your other child, the one who's really feeling the loss of your attention.

Choose something you did together before the twins came along. For example, you might offer them their usual bedtime routine, or take them to a lesson or activity they enjoy, or watch a favourite TV show together. It would be wise to go somewhere away from the twins, so you're not tempted to check on the care they're receiving.

You needn't do anything expensive or dramatic – it's the individual attention that matters. Consider this a sacrosanct time, just for you and this particular child. Focus entirely on his or her interests and accomplishments and enjoy your time together, without reference to the twins – or, for that matter, to any other siblings.

Sharing one-to-one time with your other child is one of the best ways possible to help them develop good self-esteem and to encourage them to bond positively with their twin siblings. Remain alert to their need to be considered important in their own right. Paradoxical as it may seem, *not* demanding that your other child spends time with the twins, and *not* praising that child excessively when they help out with the twins, is the best approach.

It really cannot be overstated how important it is to remind your other child or children of how special you consider them to be, especially during the first few months after the twins are born. Not only will you foster their self-confidence and sense of self-worth, but you'll also have done your best to encourage the development of positive bonds between all your children in the longer term.

Reach out for some help. There's no better favour you could ask of a friend, no more important duty you could ask of a partner, no better time to spend money on childcare.

Summary

Twins, triplets and other multiple-birth children must compete with one another for parental attention because of the similarity of their needs. At the same time, however, they will almost always share a deeply affectionate and caring bond because they've shared so many experiences. The more unalike they appear, and the more you emphasise the individuality of each of them, the less need they'll have to compete for your attention. As a result, the stronger and more positive will be the bond they form.

It's also vital to encourage a positive and enduring relationship between your twins and your other child or children. This is because twins are regarded as a great novelty, and therefore receive extra attention that's likely to make the other siblings feel jealous. Probably your greatest challenge will be to help your other children feel as special, as interesting and as important as the twins. Make it your top priority to spend time regularly with each child, and, whenever possible, to find ways for different pairs of your children to enjoy exclusive occasions together.

17
Adoption

In this chapter we'll look closely at issues arising from adopting a child, and the relationships they form with their siblings. However, while there are indeed special issues for adopting parents to consider and things you will worry about, the best you can do for your child is to 'forget' they are adopted in the first place and treat them as if they are your own biological child. Simple though it sounds, it is the only way you will build the most healthy and balanced relationship within your family.

In this chapter we'll look closely at issues arising from adopting a child, and their relationships with their siblings. Regardless of the set-up or history of how your family came about – whether you have a mix of biological and adopted children, or you've adopted a set of siblings, or you adopted a child and then chose to adopt another and are introducing the child into your established adopted family – my advice is the same.

Attitude is everything

To help me understand a bit more about how adoptive children feel, I interviewed a group of them. All are now adults, and all were adopted as babies, so they didn't remember growing up in any other family. Of course, things will be different for those who do have memories of being part of another family – I will discuss this shortly. However, one adopted child, a young woman in her mid-20s, summed up the general consensus very succinctly. She seemed surprised at first when I asked her to tell me what she thought the difference was between growing up as an adopted child and growing up as a biological child. After a pause, she replied simply, 'I really don't see any difference. Doesn't it just come down to the attitude that your parents have about you?'

My clinical experience suggests that she's right. If you expect problems, if you expect adopted children to feel somehow 'different', they probably will feel that way. If instead, you assume that you're raising them just as you would if you'd given birth to them, they'll grow up feeling like your child, just as much as any biological child feels in their family.

Age when adopted and experience before adoption

If a child is adopted before the age of about 30 to 36 months, they're unlikely to have conscious memories of their previous experiences in other circumstances. However, if they've experienced severe or repeated trauma, and in particular if this involved rejection, then whatever their age, there will be an effect. Children who've been repeatedly rejected, abused or moved from home to home will be more guarded, and will find it harder to feel certain that they're completely safe and secure. This means they'll find it more challenging than other children to open their hearts fully to others, and to make relationships without conditions with you or their siblings. They're also likely to test those relationships more often than other children – in other words, they may misbehave and test house rules more often than children from less tumultuous backgrounds, as if to make sure these relationships and boundaries are secure and 'for real'.

Adopting older children is more challenging than adopting babies, particularly when their early experiences were difficult. However, such children are likely to be incredibly determined and resilient individuals. Therefore, if you can remain patient and work through their frequent challenges without letting your boundaries slip, it may be the most rewarding thing you ever do. Furthermore, the relationships they make with their siblings, whether those siblings are your biological children or other children you've adopted, will be at least as important – probably more important – in their lives as they will be in the lives of other children who've had a more peaceful start to their life.

Adopting sibling groups

Fortunately, it's now widely recognised that it's better for sibling groups who are being considered for adoption to remain with their siblings if at all possible, rather than being adopted into different families. Of course in many ways this means a much greater workload for adopting parents than taking on just one child. However, in another sense, there's less work. Sibling groups who are being considered for adoption have almost certainly been through a great deal of change, but they've had one constant – each other. Their bond will be strong already, and they'll gain huge comfort when they're in the presence of one another.

Of course, it's just as important in this situation as in any other in which there are several children in the family that you try to treat each child fairly and to meet the individual needs of each as best you can. When they've been adopted well after birth, you'll have more to learn, and you'll have to learn it much faster, than parents who have raised their children from birth. Nonetheless, it may be easier than you think because you'll be able to count on the feeling of stability these children will have because they're with their siblings.

If you adopt one sibling group and you already have other children, you can't reasonably expect them to feel equally bonded to their step-siblings when you compare those bonds to those they've forged with the siblings they've grown up with. However, you can – and you must – expect everyone to respect one another equally, because each is an equal member of your family.

Families with biological and adopted children

This situation is the greatest challenge for parents, particularly in those situations when a biological child is born to parents who adopted because they thought they would never have a biological child. In theory, this should be no different from having all adopted or all biological children. In reality, however, parents in this situation find it almost impossible not to assess and reassess whether they're treating everyone fairly, worrying that they might be giving preferential treatment to a child of one status (biological) or the other (adopted). Under these circumstances, even more than in any other in this chapter, it will be invaluable to have someone you can talk to about your worries whenever you feel the need – a relative or friend who lives nearby, someone who's on hand to share in some of the family experiences and observe your interactions. Alternatively, you might ask your GP if there are any relevant support groups you can join.

Almost certainly, you'll be doing a great job and you will treat each child according to their needs as opposed to their origins. If, however, there's someone you can rely on to reassure you honestly, you'll feel much less anxious. Everyone will then feel calmer and happier, and your children will have little, if any, reason to feel jealous of one another. As a result, everyone will get on more easily.

If there are both biological children and adopted children in the family, it's incredibly important that you don't overcompensate, and over-protect the adopted children when there's a dispute between siblings. This is the surest way to encourage resentment and bullying behaviour. Treat each child equally when resolving arguments, and involve them both when helping them solve their dilemmas.

When you talk to your adopted children about how you love them, there's no 'more' or 'less' loving just because they were adopted. Love is not a quality that can be quantified. Therefore, you love all your children equally. It's especially important that you remind them of this, often, if you also have biological children, because they might wonder if the lack of a biological connection makes them less valuable to you.

Adolescence and identity

Adolescence is a time when your child may wish to seek their biological parents and, if they have any, their biological and/or step-siblings. This is an incredibly testing time, both for you and for your other children, because not only are they suggesting that they wish to look elsewhere to find their 'family', but also because – in moments when hormonal shifts can stir up strong emotions – they may accuse you of not being their 'real' parents anyway, and their brothers and sisters not being their 'real' family.

Try not to react. Your family is their rock and their security, and deep down, they know this. But at the same time, it's reasonable that they wish to learn as much as possible about their background, about where and whom they've come from. Encourage their search and help them as much as you can. At the same time, ignore comments about your parenting skills, but insist they behave civilly to you and to other family members.

Their reaction, if they do meet up with biological parents and siblings, will be completely unpredictable. Some children meet once, but then not again – with or without ever giving you any explanation. Many of them meet and initially feel very powerfully that they want to continue meeting. A lasting and close connection is not, however, the norm. That's because the depth of a relationship is determined more by frequency and duration of shared experience than it is by biology.

However, if your adopted child does start meeting up regularly with biological relatives, encourage them. Let your adopted child know you're available if they wish to talk through their feelings, but resist the urge to question them. Remember, love cannot be quantified, so the love they have for their biological relatives can't be 'measured' against the love they have for you and their siblings. If they now have more people they can turn to, this can only be good news. After all, the greater the number of good relationships they have in their lives, the better.

The worst outcome for your adopted child is if their biological relatives do not wish to meet up. This will no doubt feel like the most powerful of rejections. It took great courage for them to reach out, to try to initiate contact. Therefore, a rebuff – whatever the reason – will feel devastating. Don't rush in to try and soothe or 'fix' things. Make sure, however, that you're on hand if and when they wish to talk about what happened. Listen, and try not to judge anyone in this situation. Simply reassure your child that you and the rest of the family love them and will always be there for them.

While all this is going on, don't forget that your other children may not find it easy to accept the hurtful comments or to understand the new behaviours from your adolescent child as readily as you can. Make time when you can talk, either with each child individually or with everyone all together, whichever you feel is best, so you can listen to their concerns and reassure them that they've done nothing wrong, that their brother or sister still loves them but that part of growing up involves learning as much as you can about your background.

The more often you react in a calm and matter-of-fact way, the less impact this phase will have on family relationships. The negativity will pass, and given time and patience, everyone will get on well once more.

Summary

Adoption can be a wonderful experience. You choose to take someone into your family, someone you can't possibly second guess, and you have the privilege of watching them develop.

The adopted children in your family are able to develop bonds with their siblings that are just as strong and positive as the bonds would be if all your children were your biological offspring. This is the case whether every child is adopted – each from a different background – whether you adopt sibling groups, or whether you enjoy a 'rainbow family'.

You don't need a list of suggestions or guidelines that are any different from those I've already given you for raising biological children. To maximise the chances that adopted children will bond well with their siblings, your attitude is the key to everything. Treat them all as equals, and consider your family to be the most secure base possible for each family member, regardless of background. As a result, the trust between you all will strengthen and endure.

18

Divorce and separation

Divorce rates in the UK, although distressingly high, appear to have levelled off over the last five years at about 42%. However, this masks the full story, because we don't have figures for the number of cohabiting couples who also separate every year.

The most common age when a couple divorces is between 40 and 44 years, the age when many of us are quite likely to have young children living at home with us. Statistics for 2013 verify this: in that year, 48% of divorcing couples had at least one child under 16 living at home. This means, sadly, that a huge number of children have to cope with parental separation or divorce every year.

In this chapter, we'll consider how divorce and separation affect children and, in particular, whether children who have siblings living with them find it easier or more difficult to cope when their parents split up. We'll also consider the effect, if any, that marital breakup has on sibling relationships.

How divorce and separation affect children

Change is stressful for any of us. However, it feels even more upsetting if we have no clear idea about what that change will mean, or exactly when it's going to happen. That's why, although no child wants their parents to split up, they'll often say they were relieved when it finally happened. The uncertainty had begun to feel unbearable.

Even before the split actually happens, children are already on edge, anxious and frightened because they can no doubt sense the tension and discord between their parents. Children are far savvier than parents realise. Even when parents think they're hiding their feelings and shielding their children from their arguments, their children – even when very young – almost always know they're unhappy, and that they're not getting on.

A child's anxiety ratchets up, and can even cause them to suffer full-blown panic attacks, if parents involve them in their arguments, or entreat them to 'take sides'. Children are loyal to both parents, no matter how distant one of them has been or how badly that parent has behaved, so they feel impossibly conflicted when asked to assign 'blame' or 'choose' one parent over another. Their most common reaction, sadly, is to blame themselves, to feel that somehow these disagreements and all the uncertainties are their fault.

Children's reactions when parents split up

At different ages – or, more precisely, at different levels of cognitive development – children react differently to parental conflict, separation or divorce.

Young children under about six or seven years of age feel both anxious and guilty when their parents argue. During these early years, children are still egocentric. This means that they see the world most readily from their own point of view, but not so readily from the viewpoint of anyone else. They also assume that they're the cause of external events and as a result they take responsibility for what happens. So, if their parents are unhappy and angry, if they're arguing constantly, the child assumes that it must be their own fault, that the discord is because of something they did wrong. Common reactions include regressive behaviours, for example sucking their thumb if they'd stopped, or wetting their pants if they're already potty trained. They're likely to have sleep disturbances that may include nightmares, waking in the night, and/or an inability to go to sleep at bedtime. They'll seek constant reassurance from their parents, and they may be reluctant to leave the house or to be left at school or nursery. Their concerns focus more on the moment than on the future, because it's not easy for them to imagine what might happen if their parents do separate. They simply feel anxious, guilty and frightened because they sense the tension and because they have no idea what will happen next.

Older children, particularly those who are adolescent or pre-adolescent, will also feel highly anxious. However, their fears about an uncertain future – and this is something they will think about and speculate about – are usually expressed as anger. They may sulk, or have sudden and apparently unprovoked outbursts of pure fury. They may 'act out' – deliberately break house rules or get themselves into trouble at school, or even with the law. Boys in particular are liable to behave aggressively, but both boys and girls may become irresponsible, reckless, unpredictable, and appear to be out of control. Some adolescents turn their anger and fear inwards. As a result they may become depressed, feel hopeless about the future, and suffer low self-esteem. Once the separation occurs or the arguing stops, they may appear to settle down. However, if one parent moves out, they're likely to miss and idealise that parent, even if they hadn't felt particularly close to them before the separation.

If the adolescent is no longer living at home, the effects of separation and divorce appear to be somewhat less powerful. There is, however, a reliable exception. If the adolescent has just left home, for example to start university or another type of further education, they're quite likely to feel overwhelmed with anxiety, and they may even become depressed. I've seen this so often in my university clinics. The young person usually concludes that their parents were 'just waiting' for them to leave home so they could split up. They feel they now have no 'home' to return to, and that furthermore, they must 'rewrite' their history, reinterpret what was happening between their parents before they left home. This is an incredibly painful and difficult process, especially because they're trying to adjust to a new and more independent life at the same time.

The effects of divorce and separation on sibling relationships

Does having a sibling or siblings make it easier for a child to cope if their parents split up? It seems that it does. Tracy Kempton and her colleagues in the USA interviewed 77 adolescents whose parents were divorced, as well as their teachers and mothers. The adolescents had either a younger sibling or an older sibling, or was an only child. Teachers reported that the adolescents who had a sibling – younger or older – showed fewer behavioural problems than those who had no sibling.

A number of researchers, particularly in the USA, have interviewed adults whose parents separated when they were young. Their work provides overwhelming evidence that having a sibling helps both young children and adolescents cope when their parents separate. Shirley McGuire, now Senior Vice Provost at the University of San Francisco, has spent many years looking at the ways children cope with marital discord and separation. The children and adolescents she's interviewed have said repeatedly how much they relied on their siblings to help them get through parental separation. Many say that this negative experience actually strengthened their bond with their siblings.

Paige Herrick at Baylor University interviewed 263 young adults and asked them to name the one experience that served as a positive turning point in their relationship with a sibling. One of the most commonly reported events was parental separation. The adults who were interviewed also reported increased feelings of trust and closeness with their sibling when they turned to one another during parental separation.

It seems, then, that the effects of parental divorce and separation – a negative and distressing experience – can be mitigated when siblings turn to one another for support and comfort. It's interesting that very often, when siblings go through parental separation, the nature of their relationship changes. Not only do they feel closer, but the bond – even if it was originally one of equals or near-equals – becomes much more of a caring/cared-for relationship, with one sibling assuming responsibility for the wellbeing of another. In a longitudinal study looking at the effects of divorce on children, Judith Wallerstein and her colleagues at the University of California, Berkeley, interviewed 131 children every five years for 25 years. They found that very often, one child, usually the eldest, assumed a parental role, taking over the care of the younger children in the family.

Of course, siblings aren't always kind to one another during parental separation. Sometimes they will turn the anger and frustration they're afraid to show towards their parents on to a sibling. Overall, however, their interactions are more often positive than negative. Whatever else, their interactions almost always become more intense and, as you know, the intensity of emotions expressed is correlated with the strength of the resulting relationship.

Thus, whether it becomes a more positive and close relationship or a more negative and challenging one – and overwhelmingly, it is the former – the sibling relationship is strongly affected by parental separation and plays an important role in lessening the pain that the children suffer.

If you are undergoing or planning to undergo a separation, it's therefore extremely important to consider how best to help your children maintain their relationship with one another during this difficult process.

How separating parents can help their children cope

The single most important way you and your partner can help your children feel calmer and better able to cope is not to argue in their presence. The best places to discuss disagreements are public places, for example a coffee shop or restaurant, where you're more likely to remain civil, or in the presence of an objective professional such as a Relate counsellor or a mediator. At home, your role is not to argue but to co-parent. You may no longer love one another, but it's critical that you remind your children how much you both still love *them*.

A second and related point is not to criticise your partner in front of the children, and never to ask your children to take sides. No matter how aggrieved you feel towards your partner, remember that your children can never have another mother or father. Whatever has happened, they almost certainly still love you both, and they will feel themselves to be at least partly like both of you. If you criticise your partner in their presence, they take in bad feelings about themselves. This can lead to aggressive behaviour, anxiety, panic and even depression.

Third, reassure all your children, but particularly the younger ones, that what's going on between you and your partner is not their fault. Again, remind them that you both love them – they can never hear that often enough.

The relationship between your children is likely to become closer as the result of parental separation. Respect and encourage their bond, because it will help them get through the changes that separation demands. Your eldest child, and/or your eldest daughter, is likely to assume more of a protective and caring role with regard to the younger children. That's fine, but try to remain aware of how much responsibility the older one(s) is taking on. You don't want them to feel over-burdened, and it's important that they, too, have support (see Chapter 13 on over-responsibility). It will help, therefore, if you encourage them to see their friends, and/or if you make sure they each have someone they can talk to, someone outside the family, who can be more objective. Be especially aware of your own attitude to the eldest, particularly if that child is the same gender as your partner. No child should have to become a parent's confidante or supporter, especially during a separation.

Be as clear and as specific as you can, as soon as you can, about what will happen, and when it will happen. Certainty, however much upheaval it may involve, will help ease your children's anxiety. Whenever you or your partner are scheduled to spend time with your children, prioritise that commitment and make sure you see them when you promised.

When your children visit the parent they're no longer living with, try to ensure that they can visit as a group. They'll feel less anxious in the new surroundings if they have the support of each other.

Try to minimise the changes they must undergo. Small things can make a huge difference – for example, try to offer meals at the times they're used to having them. If you're the parent in new accommodation, choose the same type of bed linen for their beds that they're used to in the original family home. If they have soft toys they take to bed, or pyjamas they normally use, encourage them to bring these along when they visit. Of all times of day and night, bedtime is the time when it's most important to offer familiar surroundings and routines.

As they get older and become used to the new routines and the changed surroundings, it will help them to feel more important and responsible if you and your partner gradually start to involve them in making decisions about how and when they have contact with the parent with whom they're no longer living. At the same time, however, continue to encourage them to have contact with both parents. Try to arrange the visits so they can all go together. And, most important, stick to the arrangements that have been agreed.

Summary

Nowadays, divorce and separation are common, and many children will have to endure this painful process. The best ways to minimise the pain are not to argue in front of your children, to reassure them often that you and their other parent still love them and always will, and to offer them clarity and predictability about contact with parents and grandparents, and about any other changes they will need to face.

Throughout the process of separation and divorce – and almost certainly for many years thereafter – siblings are highly likely to turn to one another for solace and support. Make sure that this is as easy as possible for them.

19

Introducing step-siblings

The number of stepfamilies is rising steadily. In the UK, it's currently estimated that between nine and 11% of families are now stepfamilies, and one in three of us is either a stepchild, a step-parent, or a step-grandparent.

The most common configuration of the step-family is a mother, her child or children, and a stepfather. The stepfather is likely to have children who visit and who probably stay with the family, either on a regular basis or only occasionally, for example at Christmas.

A popular term for this new type of family is the 'blended' family. I will not be using this term because I think it's misleading. Step-families rarely blend, and there's almost never the smooth consistency in relationships between members of a step-family that this term suggests. The formation of good, comfortable relationships among children, stepchildren, parents and step-parents can occur when the parent–step-parent teams invest plenty of patience, love and good management, it's true. But even then, some luck is needed as well. Making a stepfamily work is hard. I've never seen one simply 'blend'!

To encourage the best relationships possible between children and stepchildren, and to make sure sibling relationships remain robust and positive, you're going to need enormous tenacity, patience, tolerance, and a concerted determination always to settle disputes and disagreements fairly. That said, spending time with step-siblings and stepchildren teaches individuals to become more tolerant, and to look at life from new and often very different viewpoints. It's probably not a situation that most of us would choose. It is, however, one that very few regret once having known it.

I will not be referring to any academic studies in this chapter, because there is so little work to draw on, even though step-families are nothing new. In fact, they were incredibly common, say, 100 years ago, because mothers so often died in childbirth and fathers then remarried. The modern stepfamily, however, is constructed on quite a different basis than it was in previous generations, based on attitudes and customs that are relatively recent. Thankfully, women in the West are no longer dying in childbirth as often as once they did,. However, many men and women nowadays decide to separate and go their own ways for a number of different reasons, often finding new partners and establishing new families along the way. According to the ONS, the average length of a marriage in the UK is now 11.5 years, with the highest rates of divorce occurring between four and eight years after a couple marries. Given our increasingly long lifespans, this isn't very long.

Experts are, therefore, steering through unchartered waters when we try to suggest ways to create harmony in the modern family set-up. However, although there are as yet few guidelines based on academic research, I and other clinicians have learned a great deal from family members in our clinics as we've tried to help them find new arrangements that can work well, often without the benefit of either previous experience or of good role models.

In this chapter I will, consequently, be referring primarily to clinical experience rather than relying on the results of academic research.

What are the main pressures on the modern step-family?

We know that during divorce and separation, one of the most powerful stresses on children is the uncertainty about their future, about who will be living where, with whom and when the changes will take place.

These stresses multiply when a step-parent, possibly with stepchildren in tow, is introduced.

Living with a new adult also introduces new house rules and different ways of going about the daily routines. Furthermore, children very often find themselves moving back and forth between two different set-ups and two different sets of rules. Especially at first, this is incredibly confusing and exhausting.

Amid all this change, there is often only one constant for a child, and that is their siblings. This is why it's so important to try to ensure that a child visits the other household together with their siblings. At times, their siblings will be their only steady point of reference. One of the most challenging situations is, therefore, when an only child suddenly acquires step-siblings.

Think back to Chapter 10 about the arrival of a new baby, and add into the mix potential teenage hormones and years of being the sole child in the home. Only children tend to be cognitively mature for their age, so they usually understand logically what's going on. However, they'll feel just as distressed as any other child, but they won't have the benefit of sibling support to help them through. Therefore, while they're trying to adjust to the new circumstances, try to ensure that there's someone 'safe and neutral' that your only child can talk to – the parent of a friend, or an aunt, uncle or grandparent.

A second stress on children is that now they very often have to share the attention of one or both parents with other children. It's been difficult enough to accept the loss of easy access to one of their parents. Now, when they do get that access, they often have to share that parent's attention with other children they hardly know. Once again, the presence of their siblings, a constant they can still count on, can be so reassuring.

Crowding and 'territory' are further stresses. The amount of living space rarely increases after a separation – often, in fact, both parents move somewhere less spacious. Add in more people, and it starts to feel particularly crowded. When humans, or any mammals for that matter, feel crowded, they're more likely to behave aggressively. Therefore, be prepared rather than surprised if this happens.

A child's position in the family may also be threatened when stepchildren visit, especially if they come to live with them. This will feel most threatening to the eldest child in a family, if they are now no longer 'first'. Similarly, the youngest may no longer be centre stage as the baby in the family. Again, thank heavens for their siblings, in relation to them, their position in the family is the same as ever it was.

Finally, a child's normal routines may be disrupted, either when they visit their other parent or when stepchildren come to stay with them. At times, it's an almost impossible challenge for parent and step-parent to ensure that everyone can still attend their clubs or lessons, get to friends' birthday parties (and remember to bring a gift), or even to make sure that homework is completed. Compromise is the only solution, and that may not be welcomed. Children who have been through a separation and are missing both one of their parents as well as their normal routine may react powerfully to what they regard as further disruption, and further curtailment of their usual way of living.

What, then, can parents and step-parents do to minimise the stress and the chaos, and try to create opportunities for children and stepchildren to create positive relationships?

Guidelines for parents and step-parents

Be clear and specific when making plans

Set out clear timetables detailing who visits whom, when, and for how long. Stick to these arrangements as a top priority, and inform all children (and adults) concerned as far ahead of time as possible.

Be clear about the house rules

Make sure everyone knows the house rules. It might be wise to reiterate any important rules each time children and stepchildren are together. It's better that they feel bored with your insistence on repetition than that they forget the limits. Ignore any complaints that this 'isn't how we do it at home'. This *is* how we do it here.

Support your partner

Always, always back up your partner when enforcing the house rules in the presence of the children, even if you don't agree at the time (as long, of course, as everyone is safe). Later, away from the home, you can discuss any disagreements about the rules or their interpretation, but never within earshot of the children. In their uncertainty in these new situations, they will naturally be looking for weaknesses in the system. Clarity and consistency are the best ways to deal with uncertainty, and the best way to reduce everyone's stress levels.

Blaming is not allowed

When there are disputes and disagreements – and there will be – do *not* ascribe blame. Resolving a dispute means finding the fairest solution for everyone concerned, and each child is to be considered as equally important as the others. Impartiality and the absence of blame are the keys that will allow each child to feel that they've received fair treatment.

Everyone needs an 'own space'

Ensure that everyone has their own area, however small, that is for them alone. This helps reduce any feelings of overcrowding. If that space is too small or too open to allow the child some privacy if they wish to have a cry and/or to feel truly alone, you might want to create a 'time out' space in the house that anyone can use. Make sure that you or your partner regulates access to that space, so any child using it can feel reassured that no one will come in and disturb them when they're taking time out.

Minimise change

Try not to change the sleeping arrangements of the children who normally live with you when stepchildren come to visit. That way, they'll feel less resentful of the visitors, and safe and secure that there is an element of familiarity. Similarly, ensure if you can that the visiting children sleep and keep their things in the same place every time they visit. That way, your home will feel increasingly familiar.

Get outdoors

Do things outdoors as often as possible. It always feels less crowded when we're outside. Furthermore, potential conflict about who has the right to what territory goes away while you're outside, because you'll be in spaces that don't belong to any of you. Even the garden feels less 'owned'.

Keep siblings together

Encourage siblings to spend time together and to enjoy one another's company. At the same time, do *not* insist that children and stepchildren do things together. Remember, they did not choose to be 'related'. This was imposed on them by you and your new partner. Instead, regard any occasion when they choose to enjoy each other's company as a real treat – and be sure to tell them so. Thank them for particular acts of kindness, for example, 'Jack, that was so nice of you to lend William that DVD, and William, I noticed how warmly you thanked him. That's great!' If you're specific like this, it increases the chance that you'll see other positive interactions when that or a similar occasion arises again.

Don't expect instant results

Most important of all, be patient! Shirley McGuire, who has interviewed a great number of children who have grown up in families with separated parents, once commented that she believes it takes at least six years before an outsider could no longer know whether they are observing a family or a stepfamily – and even that figure will depend on the ages of the children concerned, and how often they're together.

What happens to birth order when you introduce step-siblings?

You might think that if step-siblings are introduced into a family, each child will assume a 'new' birth order position, and go on to develop the characteristics of that new position. In fact, this rarely happens.

What does happen, however, is that all the children in the 'new' family will temporarily become much more competitive – and probably more aggressive – as they vie for parental attention. At the same time, the children in each of the two 'sub-families' will intensify their bonds and do everything in their power to differentiate themselves from their new 'rivals'.

This situation will settle over time, but it may feel as if that time is passing very slowly! Parents and step-parents can help if they take care to distribute their attention even-handedly and to mete out justice fairly. Even with the greatest skill in the world, however, siblings and step-siblings are never likely to feel as close to one another as they will to the siblings they knew from birth. Accept this with equanimity, and everyone will feel calmer.

Finally, it's worth noting that there is one set of circumstances when children do take on additional characteristics of their 'new' birth order position. This is when the step-siblings are introduced when the children are still quite young – under about four years of age – and they all live together. This is because we establish the foundations of our identity between the ages of about three and six years.

Summary

Overall, the introduction of a step-parent and stepchildren can be an enriching experience for your children. It teaches tolerance, comfort in the face of frequent change, and the ability to live with compromise. It's also likely to strengthen sibling bonds, because a child's relationship with their own siblings remains a constant whether the stepchildren are on hand or not.

If you're determined to be fair and even-handed with everyone, if you encourage good relationships where you see them but never insist on them where you don't, you may one day enjoy a relaxed atmosphere, even though almost no one in your 'family' is a blood relation. If you manage this, you will have riches indeed.

20

A gifted child in the family

What does it mean to be 'gifted'? There's no universally accepted definition, but I think one of the best is that offered by the National Association for Gifted Children in the USA. Gifted children, they write, 'are those who demonstrate outstanding levels of aptitude (exceptional ability to reason and learn) or competence (documented performance of achievement in top 10% or rarer) in one or more domains'.

These 'domains' are defined in an interesting way – any structured area of activity that has its own symbol system, for example maths, language and music; and any set of sensorimotor skills such as painting, sport or dance.

As you can see, even this definition – one that tries very hard to be precise – leaves itself open to interpretation and to a resetting of boundaries. It's really important to understand this. 'Gifted' is a relative concept, and when you accept that the boundaries are actually somewhat fluid, then and only then will you be able to use the term 'gifted' constructively if you're thinking of applying it to any of your children.

The truth is that everyone is gifted in some way, and one of the most important quests in life for each of us is to discover our own special talent, the way in which we're most likely to be considered gifted. Some – in particular musical talent, because this ability shows itself earlier than do most other talents – will be discovered early on in life. Others may not become apparent for many years.

The problem with giftedness is that whenever a child appears to have found theirs, those around them may feel that it's necessary to encourage them to express that gift right away, to work to excel at it and to become noticed for it. Parents who have a gifted child therefore must face an almost impossible dilemma. They have to try to guess what their child would most want when they grow up. Is this incredible ability to play the piano really the way they'll want to define themselves, how they'll wish to spend virtually all their time? Or would it be better to allow this talent simply to be part of their overall skills set?

I can't answer this for you. All parents of gifted children will have to answer these difficult questions in the best way they can. The only advice I can offer on this matter is that you should always try to answer that question with the child's point of view foremost in your mind, rather than thinking about your own needs for fame and attention. If you sense that your child will find true fulfilment by pursuing this one talent, and will be happy to do so in lieu of other things, then by all means do everything you can to ensure that your child can develop their gift right now.

Whatever you decide, at the same time you must also consider the wellbeing of your other children, and help all of them to develop the best relationships possible with one another. This is particularly important for two reasons.

First, if the gifted child is determined to focus on their gift, their relationship with their siblings will become incredibly important to them. That's because they'll have little, if any, time to interact with others and form friendships with their peers. Their siblings will become in effect their friendship group.

Second, because the gifted child is likely to attract a great deal of attention and admiration from others, you will need to work hard to minimise the jealousy and envy that your other children may feel about their talented sibling. At the same time, it's vital that you help each of them develop a strong sense of self-esteem, even while few people will regard them as 'gifted' like their sibling.

Is this a losing battle? Do siblings of gifted children dislike their more talented sibling no matter how hard you try to avoid this, and are these siblings highly likely to become troubled, jealous, and unhappy individuals? It seems not. Diana Chamrad and Nancy Robinson at the University of Washington interviewed the mothers and children of 366 two-child families, families where both children were aged between seven and 14. In some, one child was identified as gifted and the other was not. In others, both were identified as gifted. In still others, neither had been identified as gifted. Their results suggest that in pairs where one child is gifted, the non-gifted sibling does not show more behaviour problems than other children – in fact, many of them were described as having *fewer* behaviour problems than other children. Furthermore, their mothers described the relationships between gifted and non-gifted siblings as strong and positive; just as positive, in fact, as in other sibling pairs. This was confirmed when the children were interviewed; they, too, felt that their relationship with their gifted sibling was a very positive one.

Of course, this is only one study, although it is a good one. A substantial number of families were interviewed, and the results strongly indicated that the assumption that siblings won't get along if one of them is gifted is just that – an assumption.

Therefore, if there's a gifted child in your family, it is entirely possible for your children to enjoy strong and supportive relationships with one another.

What parents can do to encourage strong sibling bonds when one child is gifted

The most essential thing you strive for as parents is to treat all your children fairly. Notice that, once again, I did *not* suggest that you treat them equally. Treating each child fairly is not about making sure you spend equal amounts of time or money on each child. Treating them fairly means taking the time, on a regular basis, to consider the dreams and desires of each of your children, as well as the particular needs and challenges each of them faces, and then to try your best to help them meet their needs, to solve the problems they face, and to realise their dreams and potential. You must do this without regard to whether or not anyone else considers your child's expression of their talents to be 'exceptional'. This means, of course, that you'll want to spend some time with each child on a regular basis, so you get to know each as fully as possible.

There are five more elements to consider when fostering a fair relationship between your children.

1. Help them in all aspects

Try as best you can to spend at least as much time helping your children cope more effectively in areas where they're struggling as you spend helping them develop their talents. That way, each child has the best chance of growing up to be a balanced, well-rounded individual, of developing *all* their life skills to the best of their ability. It's so much easier, and so much more enjoyable, to help them when they're already excelling. It's at least as important, however, to help them overcome challenges and deficits in their capabilities. Balance is the best route to happiness.

2. Watch your language

Labelling children 'gifted' or 'problematic' – in other words, using loaded, all-encompassing, 'good' and 'bad' terms – is never helpful. Feel free to evaluate their *behaviour* – you might say, for example, 'You sing beautifully', or 'Let's work on your spelling, because it could be better' – but no individual deserves to be reduced to a single adjective. We're each so much more complex than that! Furthermore, when you describe behaviours instead of referring to your child's entire identity, you suggest hope and possibility. Behaviours, after all, are open to change, and can always improve.

3. Avoid comparing your children

Comparisons imply that one child is somehow 'better' while the other is 'worse'. This is not helpful. It makes the 'better' child worry that their sibling will feel envious and hostile towards them, while at the same time it could make the 'worse' child feel unworthy and unvalued in your eyes. When you compare them, you also encourage them to compete, rather than to cooperate with each other. Furthermore, children are more likely to feel in control of their lives and to develop greater self-confidence if you praise them for their effort, rather than if you focus on any prizes they 'win' at the expense of others who must therefore be considered as 'losers'.

4. Help each of your children find their gift

Your expectation that each child has a gift makes it clear to them that each is equal in your eyes. As a result, they won't feel threatened by the achievements of their siblings. You will have given them no need to compete with one another.

5. Expect them to do well

Finally, in whatever areas your children hope to do well, assume that this is exactly what will happen. When those around us expect us to succeed, we're far more likely to do so, as Robert Rosenthal and Lenore Jacobson showed in their now famous 'Pygmalion effect' experiment.

Treating all your children as gifted

In 1966, Rosenthal and Jacobson tested children in 18 classrooms in a California primary school at the beginning of the school year. The test they used, the Test of General Ability, is a standard IQ test. However, in order to create higher expectations, the researchers gave the test a totally fictitious title. They referred to it as the 'Harvard Test of Inflected Acquisition', and explained that the test could measure academic 'blooming'. After scoring the tests, Rosenthal and Jacobson told the teachers that certain children in their classes had obtained scores in the top 20%, and that this meant these students were ready to 'bloom', to realise their potential. They then told the teachers who these children were.

In truth, these 'bloomers' were selected completely at random – in other words, there was no difference between them and students whose names were not on the lists.

Eight months later, the researchers returned to the school and tested all the children again using the same test. The results? The students who had been described as 'ready to bloom' showed greater IQ gains that those who had not been labelled in this way. Although the effect was less powerful for older children (aged 11 and 12), younger children who had been labelled 'bloomers' (particularly those aged five to seven) showed a significant improvement in their IQ score.

Summary

When you truly believe your children can realise their dreams and potential, particularly when they're young, something happens – either within them, or as a result of the way you react to and observe them, or both – that increases the chance that this belief will become a reality.

It will cost you nothing except an attitude of mind to give your children the best chance possible to realise their dreams. Simply believe that each is gifted in some way, and set out to discover how. Not only are they more likely to feel self-confident, they'll also have no reason to feel envious of their siblings' 'gifts', and so are likely to enjoy normal healthy relationships with them.

21

A sibling with special needs

'Special needs' can mean many things. A child may be normal at birth and develop completely normally, but then sustain an injury or be involved in an accident that causes permanent damage. A child may be normal at birth and later develop a chronic or life-threatening illness such as leukaemia. Or they may have an illness from birth, for example cystic fibrosis. Their affliction may be physical – cerebral palsy is one example – or cognitive and/or social – for example autism or Down's syndrome.

Overall, a child with special needs (I will also refer to them as the 'target child' in this chapter) is one who is either unable to reach expected goals or milestones given their chronological age, or unable to be involved (without extensive help) in activities that are considered to be normal for their age, or both. In this chapter we'll look at the effect this has on sibling relationships within the family.

General effects

The effects on sibling relationships will depend on the ages of the children in question. There are, however, some general, more universal aspects that will affect siblings of all ages when one child in the family has special needs.

The first is the number of children in the family. The larger the family, the less impact there is on well siblings of having a brother or sister with special needs. This makes sense, because in larger families there will be more children who can help out. Larger families carry another benefit as well. When there is more than one well child in the family, research suggests that they find comfort and support in one another. Bonds between the well children appear to be strong and positive, presumably because they work together to share responsibility for helping with the child who needs it, and, in doing so, they become good friends. Research also shows that if they're girls – this isn't necessarily the case for boys – they're more likely than their peers to go into caring professions when they're older.

The second important factor is *when* the target child is diagnosed. If the disability occurs later in childhood, as the result of an injury or late-onset illness for example, there will have been time for that child to develop normal relationships with their siblings. Under these circumstances the sibling relationships in the family tend to be more equal, rather than solely a caring/cared-for relationship, as is more often the case when the target child's disability was present from birth. This means that during times of turbulence – for example when one sibling enters adolescence – the bond between the well children and the target child is less likely to be disrupted, because the relationship is based on a number of factors rather than just on caring and being cared for.

The age difference between the target and the well siblings makes a difference, as does the direction of that age difference. The closer the two are in age, the more rivalry and conflict there will be between them because, even if one is slower to develop, they'll still have many of the same needs at the same time. This can be particularly challenging for parents when the children are young. When a well child isn't capable of understanding that their sibling needs special attention or more attention, they'll react jealously, having tantrums or striking out at the target child. If they remember these incidents when they're older, this may give rise to guilty feelings, even though it was perfectly understandable at the time. If the well child is the elder, they'll almost always assume a caring role. However, whether the well child is younger or older, parents may unconsciously expect much more of them, both as helps and as if to 'make up' for what the target child cannot achieve – although the latter is neither universal, nor, when it does occur, is the intent malicious or even conscious. Neither over-responsibility nor compensatory achievement is a helpful pressure. Both cause the well child to feel anxious and resentful of their sibling.

If a child with special needs is competent either cognitively or socially (social competence is the more important), their siblings will find it easier to get along with them. They'll also be more likely to want to help the target child, and to try to create a lasting relationship with them.

If the target child's behaviour is highly aggressive, or bizarre or socially unacceptable in some way, the others are less likely to want to form a close relationship with them. This becomes especially important if the target child attends the same school as their siblings, even if they're in a special unit in that school. The fear of being teased by their peers for having a 'weird' brother or sister is likely to mean that they'll try hard to distance themselves from their sibling, particularly during adolescence.

However, later on, many well children say they're glad they shared their upbringing with their less able sibling. When they become adults, many individuals who have a sibling with special needs say that they're grateful to have had the privilege of looking after them. They say it has made them more compassionate, more grateful for their own good health, more likely to notice if someone needs help, and more willing to reach out to others generally. One study noted that there's less conflict between sibling pairs if one of the pair has special needs. We can't know from this observation whether that's because parents insist that well siblings show tolerance, or whether the children notice themselves that their sibling is less able and react altruistically to them of their own accord. I suspect both factors contribute.

These factors cut across all sibling bonds when one child in the family has special needs. In addition, there are some specific types of interaction between well and target siblings that depend on their age.

Age-dependent factors

When children are young – under about seven years of age – they will find it difficult to understand what's wrong with their brother or sister. When they're very young, they may not even appear to notice the disability.

They do, however, notice the loss of attention from their parents, and they definitely notice if the target sibling is getting more attention than they are. As a result, they may behave aggressively towards the target child. More often, however, they will either exhibit regressive behaviour – wetting themselves if they're toilet trained already, or throwing tantrums, for example – or they'll imitate some of the target sibling's behaviours. This is not meant to mock; it's simply a bid for more parental attention. As they grow older and become able to understand that their sister or brother really does need the extra help they're given, they're likely to bid for parental attention more adaptively, by offering to help. As a consequence – that is, if parents don't demand too much from them or ask them to help in ways they can't readily manage – the bond between the siblings will strengthen.

Not all children, however, become closer to the target sibling as they become better able to understand what's wrong. A few may instead withdraw into themselves and become completely unable or unwilling to ask for help from parents when they need it, because they feel that their 'need' is so unimportant compared to their sibling's needs. This is especially true if the target child's strength and abilities are deteriorating, if for example they have a terminal illness. It's a big thing to ask during such distressing times, but it's really important that, if you're in this unhappy situation, you offer some special times, some desired one-to-one attention, to well siblings when one of your children is very ill. If you don't do this, or if circumstances prevent you, there's a danger that later on, your well siblings will suffer from low self-esteem and low self-worth.

Even if the relationships between all your children are strong and positive, they may be challenged when a well sibling enters adolescence. This is a time of heightened self-awareness and heightened self-criticism, and the time when the desire to be accepted by peers is greatest. In their fear of being considered 'odd' through association with their sibling, the young adolescent may openly reject the target child. This apparently sudden, unprovoked change in attitude may be incredibly hard for their brother or sister to understand. The target child's siblings are often some of the only friends they have, so they'll feel not only rejected, but isolated and lonely as well. Parents can try to help by explaining what's going on to the target child, and by encouraging the well sibling to consider the impact of their behaviour on their brother or sister. But whatever you do, adolescence is still likely to be a tricky time. Be patient, and try to be a good role model for your adolescent.

The importance of the relationship between siblings once they're adults depends almost entirely on your expectations and the patterns you encourage them to establish when they're young. If you expected all family members to make a reasonable contribution to the care of the target sibling, but at the same time you gave time and importance to each family member, then adult siblings are highly likely to continue to maintain a positive relationship with the target sibling, and to continue to help them.

There's one other interesting factor that contributes to the closeness of the bond when the siblings are adults. It seems that *where* the target 'child' lives once they become an adult will affect the frequency of visits from their well siblings. If that sibling continues to live with their parents, as the majority of them do, their siblings – particularly sisters – are likely to visit their brother or sister more often than if the target sibling is living in residential care or independently.

Wherever the sibling with special needs lives as an adult, they will almost certainly rate the relationship with their well siblings as incredibly important to them, a major determinant of their wellbeing. The well siblings almost always consider that growing up with a brother or sister with special needs was an extremely valuable experience for them, that it made them more caring and considerate of others. They are, however, unlikely to consider the relationship itself to be as important to them as it is to the target sibling.

When one sibling has special needs

By now you've no doubt realised that the most important determinant of a good sibling relationship in *any* family is that parents take time to value each child as an individual. Such behaviour, however, becomes even more important when one of your children has needs that require you to spend more time caring for that child than for the others.

Thus, although your commitment to your child with special needs may be immutable, the quality and content of the time you spend with your other children can more than compensate for the lack of time you have to offer them. Therefore, no matter how busy you are, make sure you spend some enjoyable one-to-one time with each of your children every week, doing or talking about something that's really important to them.

It's also crucial that family members feel free to talk openly about the problems faced by the target child and, as a consequence, the entire family. A study conducted by Dr Mandy Byron at London's Great Ormond Street Hospital for Children showed that relationships between siblings are better, closer and more positive when there have been open discussions in the family about the challenges with which they must deal. Byron interviewed a number of families in which one of the children suffered from cystic fibrosis. Talking about the disorder, as well as feeling free to voice their own feelings, was correlated with greater feelings of satisfaction for all the children in the family. Byron also noted how happy the well siblings felt whenever someone asked after their health and enquired about their interests, rather than always asking only about the health of their brother or sister.

It therefore follows that you can also help fortify the relationships between your children if you ask relatives and friends to pay special attention to well siblings, perhaps even to bring them a small token whenever they bring a gift for the target child. When the others feel equally valued, they won't feel as threatened by the extra attention bestowed on their brother or sister.

It's also important that there are regular occasions when your well children can talk to you about what's wrong with their sister or brother, and what might happen to them. It's extremely important that you're always open and honest, but that at the same time you remain sensitive to how much they're ready to take on board. It's better to ask them what they wish to know, rather than to volunteer information they may not be ready to hear. Remember, particularly with regard to well siblings who are less than about six years of age, to reassure them repeatedly that their sibling's condition is not their fault.

Another way to help your children feel closer is to encourage them to confide in one another, without you in attendance. This is particularly important if the target child has a serious physical illness. Clinical observations suggest that these children are often hesitant to talk to parents about how they're feeling for fear of worrying them or causing them to overprotect them. They will, however, talk more freely with their siblings and as a result, both will feel better – and closer to one another.

According to study after study, a key factor affecting sibling relationships is the attitude parents impart to their children. If you assume that everyone will play a part to help the target child to live the best life possible, if you ask each child to contribute – but only according to their ability – and if at the same time you make it clear that you value each of your children as unique individuals, your children are most likely to care for and feel close to one another. They're also likely to grow up to be self-confident, to be sensitive to the needs of others, and to be considered a valued member of their friendship groups and as a colleague at work.

Summary

It cannot be denied that a child with special needs puts added pressures on a family. At the same time, however, their presence means that everyone is likely to become more responsible and nurturing individuals – particulary towards one another – to be more aware of and grateful for their own health, and to understand the value of remaining present and strong in the face of suffering.

22

When a sibling dies

When a child dies, our hearts go out at once to the grieving parents. However, that child's brothers and/or sisters will have suffered a terrible loss as well, the loss of someone they assumed would be part of their life for ever. To make it even more devastating, this often occurs at an age when those siblings can't fully take in what has happened, or even begin to understand why.

In this chapter I want us to consider the loss of a sibling from the point of view of an often overlooked group, their brothers and sisters. This chapter is not so much about how you can help your children form and strengthen their relationships, but more about how you can help them cope with the loss of a relationship that was central to their lives, just as it was to yours.

Age of surviving siblings when their brother or sister dies

Death is a difficult concept for children to grasp. Until about the age of four, they fail to understand the irreversibility of death, and see it instead as a temporary occurrence, something that can be done and then undone. Therefore, they may think that their dead sibling has merely fallen asleep, and that they'll soon wake up again. Only gradually do children come to understand that death is a permanent condition – often, they will be nearly ten or eleven before they can truly understand that death is irreversible and universal.

Another problem, particularly for children who are less than about six years of age, is that if a sibling dies, they may feel responsible for the death. This is because before the age of about five or six, young children assume that everything happens because they made it happen or wanted it to happen. Therefore, they may worry that they caused their sibling's death, particularly if they resented them, for example if the child was ill for a long time and received a great deal of parental attention at the expense of the other children in the family.

Young children – and, occasionally, even older children – may become afraid to go anywhere near hospitals, or even doctors, if a sibling dies. They may also become frightened if they notice any similarities between themselves and the sibling who died. Some, for example, become anxious if someone comments perfectly innocently that they're looking a bit thin. They remember that their sister or brother became thin before they died, and begin to worry that they, too, may now die.

When parental time and attention is focused on a sibling who's gravely ill or who has suffered serious injuries, very young children won't be able to understand why there's so much focus on the ailing sibling, while they're virtually ignored. They'll feel left out and vulnerable, and as a result they may exhibit attention-seeking, regressive behaviours. Alternatively, they may appear to take on some of their sibling's symptoms in an effort to gain parental attention. Parents may be too overwhelmed even to notice, so the child may intensify their frantic attempts for recognition.

The older the child, the more capable they will be of understanding what's happening, and the more restrained they'll be in their bids for attention. However, they, like the adults around them, will no doubt be feeling extremely distressed, and possibly frightened about their own health. Therefore, if no one comforts or consoles them, they may conclude that their needs are trivial and of little importance. This can have long-term, lasting consequences. They may suffer from low self-esteem, and a sense of helplessness, and even be more vulnerable to recurring bouts of depression.

If the sibling is an adolescent when the death occurs, they, like young children, are likely to feel guilty. At this age, however, the guilty feelings are not because they feel responsible for the death. Instead, they may feel this way because they believe they didn't spend enough time with their sibling while he or she was still alive. Or they may feel they don't deserve to be healthy when their sibling suffered so much.

These guilty feelings and the sense of injustice can be so easily triggered during adolescence, and they may haunt them for the rest of their lives. There's a scene in the film *Walk the Line*, a film about the life of the country and western singer Johnny Cash, that demonstrates chillingly what a devastating effect guilt can have on the surviving child. Early in the film, Johnny's older brother dies in a terrible sawmill accident. This boy was obviously his father's favoured son, and in his overwhelming grief, his father turns on Johnny and shouts his despair: 'Why did he have to die? Why couldn't it have been you?' From that time on, even into adulthood, Johnny Cash suffered from repeated bouts of depression, drug dependency, and an unquenchable desire to achieve more and ever more fame. The implication is that these feelings of unworthiness stemmed from his father's reaction to the death of Johnny's brother, and his own guilt for feeling unable to measure up to his brother.

Loss of a sibling in early adulthood is, as in adolescence, a relatively rare occurrence. However, the effects at this time are also powerful and lasting, causing some surviving siblings to suffer high levels of anxiety, to experience panic attacks, and, as with adolescents, to be more vulnerable to depression. These young adults may also over-react to any unusual physical symptoms they experience, particularly if their sibling died of an illness rather than an accident. When interviewed, the most common explanation they give is that they now feel more 'vulnerable'.

As we grow old, sadly, the loss of siblings is something we increasingly have to expect and accept. That does not, however, lessen the deep sorrow that the surviving siblings feel. Victor Cicirelli, professor of psychology at Purdue University, has conducted extensive research to discover how adults feel about the loss of a sibling. When older adults talk about their loss, they often describe a feeling of 'incompleteness'. Because the relationship with our siblings extends over the whole of our life, their death may represent the loss of the only person who could share their early memories. Many older people report that the loss is so devastating that it feels as though they've lost a part of their personal identity.

Circumstances surrounding the death

When a baby dies at birth, or if the mother miscarries, the parents are just as devastated as they would be if their child had died at any other age. However, if the surviving siblings never saw or knew the baby they'll feel less affected by the death than their parents will. This is particularly true for very young children, who can't yet grasp the concept of death.

This does not mean, however, that they're not affected by the loss. Their parents' grief and withdrawal, and the consequent loss of attention, distresses them, and if they're unable to understand why their parents seem to have withdrawn, they may conclude that it's because they've done something wrong. They'll feel guilty, and like so many children who feel overlooked, they'll resort to attention-seeking and regressive behaviours.

The reaction to a miscarriage or perinatal death, therefore, depends on the age of the sibling who experiences it. Young children react to the loss of parental attention, whereas older children and adolescents understand better what's happened and grieve for the loss itself.

If a sibling dies after a long illness, their surviving siblings are highly likely to feel guilty because, naturally, they no doubt resented the child who occupied so much of their parents' time and attention. It helps if the children enjoyed a normal sibling relationship before one of them fell ill, because earlier happy memories will surface later. Just after the death, however, guilty feelings are likely to predominate. With time, surviving siblings may start to worry about their own health, particularly if they experience any symptoms that remind them of what happened to the sibling they lost. They may also suffer in silence when they're upset or worried, believing that their own concerns must be trivial compared to what their sibling suffered, or because they're afraid of worrying their parents.

If a child dies suddenly, their siblings are likely to react as they would after any major trauma. They're likely to exhibit some, if not all, symptoms of post-traumatic stress disorder (PTSD) – panic attacks, avoidance of particular places or people associated with the death, nightmares and general anxiety. There's also the increased and ongoing risk of depression and bouts of anxiety that accompanies any unexpected loss, particularly if the death occurred during the sibling's teenage years. In these circumstances, most children are overwhelmingly frightened and want an explanation, but are afraid to ask their parents because they seem so distant, so overcome by their own grief.

Finally, although a sudden death is shocking for everyone, research suggests that adolescent males who lose a brother through accident or homicide are affected most. A large proportion – some studies suggest nearly half of them – will experience full-blown PTSD. Fortunately, the worst of PTSD symptoms resolve over the following six to 12 months, generally without treatment. However, some individuals will suffer from feelings of anxiety and helplessness for the rest of their lives.

Parental reaction

This, understandably, is the most important factor that affects the surviving siblings. The more the surviving siblings are overlooked, and the more everyone around the family focuses on parental grief only, the more likely it is that the children will continue to suffer. In addition they may start to feel guilty about their anxiety and neediness, assuming that their feelings are unimportant compared to whatever their sibling suffered before they died. Teenagers and those in middle childhood in particular may begin to fear that something terrible will happen to them as well.

The longer parents grieve without taking notice of the other children, the more profound will be the effect on their surviving children. That's why, if a relative or friend notices that parents are unaware or unable to comfort their other children, they would do the family a valuable service by offering to spend time with the surviving children, comforting them and letting them talk about their worries and fears.

Another potential problem is the idealisation by parents of the dead child. Once someone is dead, they can no longer make any mistakes, and parents may forget any of the mistakes they did make or any irritating habits they may have had. It can, therefore, be all too easy to idealise a child who has died. Parents may speak of the 'perfect' child they lost, or preserve their bedroom just as it was to remind them constantly of that child when they were well. This is extremely upsetting for the surviving children, who – like Johnny Cash – may start to believe that they can never live up to this ideal.

Therefore, the sooner that all family members can share, openly and realistically, their memories of the child who has died, the sooner the surviving siblings will recover and the more likely they are to feel they're still valued and important to their parents. It's not about parents getting over their grief quicker for the sake of their other children. Rather it's about the openness and dialogue that you create within your family, which will make your grief, and theirs, easier to work through.

Focusing on the surviving siblings

The loss of a sibling is more common than most people realise. A recent study puts the figure at 5–7% in the USA. It's important, therefore, that professionals know the best way to help a family if this tragedy does occur. We still have much to learn, but we do know that it will definitely help surviving siblings recover if parents can be encouraged to comfort them and allow them to discuss their fears and worries; or, if they feel unable to do so, to find someone who will do that for them in the short term.

Attention should also be given to the surviving children's ongoing schooling and other aspects of normal life before the loss. A study by Jason Fletcher at the University of Wisconsin–Madison found that the loss of a sibling is associated with a reduction in the amount of education the surviving siblings receive, and, later on, with a lower earning capacity. They also noted that girls who lose a sibling are less likely to marry or have children, particularly if their sibling died after a long illness.

Warmth, acceptance and, most of all, time spent with grieving siblings when the death occurs might well prevent some of these adverse reactions.

There is surprisingly little research into the effect of the death of a child on the relationship between surviving siblings. It seems logical that a death would make surviving siblings more aware of the importance of spending quality time together while it's possible to do so, and therefore it would only strengthen the bonds between them. This is certainly an area that deserves further study.

Potential positive effects

The loss of a sibling is a tragic event. However, at the same time it can make those who loved and cared for them stronger and more resilient. Betty Davies at the University of British Columbia interviewed adults who had lost a sibling in early adolescence. She found that 75% of them felt they'd experienced psychological growth. They said they felt they understood the meaning of life better as a result, were imbued with a greater sense of purpose, had gained a more sensitive outlook on life, and felt more comfortable with their own mortality and with the deaths of others. They also felt proud that they had managed to survive such a terrible experience.

Siblings who are allowed to help care for a dying sibling also feel they have learned a great deal from the experience. Even when the dying child is deteriorating, siblings feel better if they know what's going on and if they can help comfort their sibling, better than if parents try to shield them from what's going on. They later report feeling more valued, both by their parents and their sibling, and they're more likely to feel empowered rather than helpless and overlooked.

What parents can do to ease surviving siblings' distress

If you lose or have lost a child, the most important thing you can do for your other children is also the most difficult in the early days after the death. You must put aside the pain of your loss so you can make an effort, on a regular basis, to show the others how much they, too, matter to you. If possible, try to allow the others to carry on with as many of their normal activities as you can manage, particularly those related to their education so that they don't fall behind.

If you feel unable to interact with your other children because you're so exhausted from coping with the loss of your child, or if you feel too overwhelmed with your own grief, ask a relative or friend to step in and give their time, some comfort, and a sense of normality to the surviving children. It's also absolutely vital to reassure them, particularly younger ones, that what's happening is not their fault.

If you can encourage all your children to participate in the dying child's care, they'll feel more valued, and they'll be less frightened because they'll know first-hand what's going on. Never force a child to do more than they feel comfortable with, but instead gently encourage them to spend time with their dying sibling and help out as much as they feel able.

It's also important to talk about what's happening both at the time and after the child dies. Do your best to respond sensitively and honestly to your surviving children's concerns.

Try, too, to avoid idealising the child who has died or to preserve their memory in unrealistic ways, ways that are likely to make the others feel inadequate. Furthermore, don't expect any of the others to compensate for your loss – each child has an equally valuable contribution to make to the family, and no one can 'make up' for anyone else.

When you feel overwhelmed, don't hesitate to ask for help, both help for your children and also help for yourself, so that you can work through your grief in a place where you feel free to 'let go'. That way, you will recover sooner and feel able to give of yourself again to your surviving children, who need you as much – if not more – than ever.

Summary

When a child dies, everyone in the family suffers. If, however, that loss is mourned openly and realistically, if the contributions from each family member are valued, and if parents do their best to show the surviving children how much they still love and value them, all the surviving family members will have gained much – even though they gained it as the result of a tragic loss.

23

A note on single children

Despite the fact that this book is about families with more than one child, I don't feel it's right to overlook single-child families. You may have picked this book up before you embark on growing your family, and want to ensure that your single child has the best start in life, before a sibling comes along. Or you may be considering, for various reasons, sticking with one child but are mindful of the impact this may have on your child. Here we'll look at what you can do to foster an environment where your child does not miss out on the positives of having siblings around them.

One-child families account for a large and growing percentage of families in the Western world. In the UK, for example, nearly 47% of families have just one child, and it's been predicted that this figure will rise to over 50% by 2023. There are a number of reasons why single-child families are becoming popular, despite the many benefits that siblings offer one another, particularly in terms of social development.

An important reason why a growing number of parents have chosen to raise only one child is because it's become socially acceptable for parents to make that choice.

Women are also now becoming more accepted as equals in the work force. I wish I could say that it's already considered to be *fully* acceptable for them to work as equals alongside men. It's not. But things have come a long way, and now, a couple can more easily choose to have just one child so both parents can continue to devote a great deal of energy to furthering their careers – particularly if they're equally willing to share childcare. There's also the increasing cost of raising children to consider, and some couples feel that if they have one child, they can provide everything they'd like to for that child while at the same time continuing to further any other interests they may have.

Now that having one child is recognised as perfectly acceptable, and now that it is generally a choice rather than a 'second best' option, parents' attitudes to their single child has changed – for the better. Parents of singles are no longer as likely to overprotect their child as they so often did years ago. Today, single children are raised much in the same way as are children in larger families, except that they never have to share the spotlight with anyone else in their family.

Parents today are well aware of how important it is that children learn how to interact skilfully with their peers. Most parents who choose to have just one understand that their child won't have the chance to learn those skills at home unless they make this happen. They therefore provide lots of opportunities for their child to mix with other children. As a result of this, as well as the fact that one-child families are no longer unusual, they're rarely seen as odd or eccentric nowadays, and they're no more likely than other children to be teased or bullied.

What, therefore, are the characteristics that are most commonly associated with children who grow up without siblings?

Assets typical of children who are raised without siblings

Only children tend to be articulate, and because linguistic development is highly correlated with academic success, they also tend to do well at school. All firstborns are exposed to more rich (adult) linguistic input because they start life enjoying full parental attention. Unlike firstborns in larger families, however, single children never have to lose that full attention and never have to share it with younger siblings. They therefore almost always acquire excellent language skills, and they do so relatively quickly.

Single children also tend to be quite logical and organised. After all, they grow up in a household surrounded by adults, and adults generally approach challenges more logically than do children. Consequently, they learn to take their time and to use logic to solve problems, rather than allowing their emotions to dominate. Furthermore, because they're not competing with any siblings for parental attention, they can learn at their leisure the best ways to solve problems as they arise.

Finally, only children are generally able to amuse themselves happily, and to spend significant amounts of time alone. As a result, they're quite self-contained whenever they need to be.

Potential problems of an only child

Only children acquire the qualities described above because they're able to enjoy a great deal of undivided attention from their parents. Nonetheless, parents can't provide them with all the skills they'll need to achieve their goal when they're grown up. We all need more than just academic and problem-solving skills to realise our dreams. Good social skills are absolutely essential. In particular, we need to know how to 'read' our peers and how to react appropriately to them. The only individuals who can teach us how to do that are children who are close in age to us while we're growing up. Siblings are the best social skills educators we'll ever have.

Living with other children teaches us to think fast, to learn to read other people's desires and intended actions, and to know how to take advantage of that knowledge. When children grow up with other children, they have to figure out how to stand up for what they want, oftenwithout the help of adults. Siblings teach each other how to be 'street smart'.

Living with other children also means that we learn to put up with disorder, and to compromise or change strategies when things don't go according to plan. Children who grow up alone don't have many opportunities to learn how to do this. They find it harder to adapt quickly and to change strategies, yet to come out ahead when faced with disorder.

What parents can do to help only children acquire 'sibling-related' skills

It's not difficult, although it does require a large investment of time, to find ways to bring lots of peer interactions into your child's life, and also to introduce them to situations that will challenge them in new and positive ways. Here are a few suggestions.

Fill your house with their friends

Encourage them to invite their friends over and to accept return invitations readily. When friends come to your home, allow the children to spend time together with only the minimal supervision to ensure their safety. When there are disputes, intervene only if you need to do so, and follow the guidelines in Chapter 9.

Challenge them physically as well as cognitively

Encourage your child to find activities that will develop their physical skills as well as their intellectual ability. This helps them not only to develop a wider skills set, but also to gain athletic prowess. The ability to excel at sport is associated with greater popularity among children and teenagers. Martial arts, dance, swimming and tennis are good all-round choices.

Make team and group activities an important part of their life

Encourage them to participate in group activities, for example team sports and drama. Learning to be part of a team will encourage them not only to develop their own skills, but also to learn how to use those skills in concert with others. A good team player is also generally more well liked.

Use holidays to advantage

Consider taking holidays with other families. That way, you'll come close to recreating a large family set-up, so peer interactions can take place more readily. It would be particularly good if at least one of the other children with whom you share your holiday is older than your child, so your child learns to get on in a new way, when they're not the leader and organiser of the group.

Summary

There are, without a doubt, wonderful advantages that come with being an only child, most particularly that the child grows up knowing they'll always be the sole focus of their parents' pride and adoration. However, only children do miss out on learning how to be 'street smart' and how to develop the widest set of social abilities. These skills are learned naturally when a child grows up with siblings.

To ensure that your single child has as many skills as possible to help them achieve their potential and realise their dreams, make sure they have plenty of opportunities to spend time with other children and to form firm friendships throughout their childhood and adolescence.

Golden rules for building positive sibling relationship

Here, in summary, are what I believe to be the seven 'golden rules' for parents who are raising more than one child:

1. Value each of your children for the unique individual he or she is. Each one deserves your unconditional love, and that makes your treatment of them equal, because love is not quantifiable. This gives them little reason to be jealous of one another.
2. Keep the communication lines open as far as possible throughout their childhood and adolescence. Get together as a family on a regular basis.
3. Be a good role model. Behave as you hope they will, and in particular show kindness and respect towards one another.
4. Regard disagreements between your children as opportunities for them to learn something, rather than as distressing problems to be avoided or minimised.
5. Establish family traditions that your children can enjoy while they're growing up, traditions they'll look back on fondly later on.
6. Find every opportunity you can to encourage teamwork and cooperation among your children.
7. Enjoy your time together as often as possible. Children grow up.

References

Books

Biddulph, Steve and Biddulph, Shaaron. *The Complete Secrets of Happy Children*. London: Thorsons, 2003.

Blair, Linda. *Birth Order*. London: Piatkus, 2011.

Blair, Linda. *The Happy Child*. London: Piatkus, 2009.

Brazelton, T. Berry. *Understanding Sibling Rivalry The Brazelton Way*. Cambridge, MA: Da Capo Press, 2005.

Cicirelli, Victor G. *Sibling Relationships Across the Lifespan*. New York: Plenum Press, 1995.

Conger, Rand D. and Elder, Glen H. Jr. *Families in Troubled Times: Adapting to Change in Rural America. Social Institutions and Social Change*. Hawthorne, NY: Aldine de Gruyter, 1994.

Devlin, Bernie, Feinberg, Stephen E., Resnick, Daniel P. and Roeder, K. *Intelligence, Genes and Success: Scientists Respond to the Bell Curve*. New York: Springer-Verlag, 1997.

Faber, Adele and Mazlish, Elaine. *Siblings Without Rivalry*. London: Piccadilly Press, 1998.

Ford, Gina. *The Contented Baby with Toddler Book*. London: Vermillion, 2009.

Gardner, Howard. *Developmental Psychology: An Introduction*. Boston: Little, Brown and Co., 1978.

Gleitman, Henry, Gross, James, and Reisberg, Daniel. *Psychology: International Student Edition*. London: W.W. Norton and Co., 2011.

Goleman, Daniel. *Emotional Intelligence: Why It Can Matter More Than IQ*. London: Bloomsbury, 1996.

Kluger, Jeffrey. *The Science of Siblings*. London: Amazon (*Time* special edn, adapted from *The Sibling Effect: What the Bonds Among Brothers and Sisters Reveal About Us*. London: Riverhead Books (Penguin Group), 2011).

Lamb, Michael E., and Sutton-Smith, Brian (eds). *Sibling Relationships: Their Nature and Significance Across the Lifespan*. London: Psychology Press, 2009.

Markham, Laura. *Calm Parents, Happy Siblings: How to Stop the Fighting and Raise Friends for Life*. London: Vermillion, 2009.

McRae, R.R. and Costa, P.T. *Personality in Adulthood: A Five-Factor Theory Perspective* (2nd edn). New York: Guildford Press, 2003.

Murray, Lynne. *The Psychology of Babies*. London: Constable and Robinson, 2014.

Parker, Jan and Stimpson, Jan. *Raising Happy Brothers and Sisters*. London: Hodder and Stoughton, 2004.

Peek, P.M. *Twins in African and Diaspora Cultures: Double Trouble, Twice Blessed*. Bloomington: Indiana University Press, 2011.

Segal, Nancy L. *Born Together – Reared Apart: The Landmark Minnesota Twin Study*. Cambridge: Harvard University Press, 2012.

Wallerstein, Judith, Lewis, Julie M. and Blakeslee, Sandra. *The Unexpected Legacy of Divorce: The 25 Year Landmark Study*. New York: Hyperion Books, 2000.

Docudrama

Amiel, Jon (director) and Wallace, Marjorie (writer). *The Silent Twins*. BBC, 1986.

Films

The King's Speech (2010, director Tom Hooper).

Walk the Line (2005, director James Mangold).

Surveys

Bounty.com, 2011: Survey of 2,116 parents to determine number and gender of children in 'happiest' families. As reported by Lisa Belkin, 'The Perfect Family' in the *New York Times,* 7 April 2011.

Eurostat: Annual Report into happiness, 2013–2014: survey of approximately 366,650 individuals across 28 EU countries plus Switzerland, Iceland, Norway and Serbia, to examine wellbeing. As reported by Harry Wallop in the *Telegraph,* 2 June 2015.

Harman, Bronwyn, 2015: Survey of 950 parents to find types of families associated with highest life satisfaction. As reported by Emma Wynne in ABC Perth News, 17 August 2015.

Articles

Akerman, Britta and Suurvee, Eve. 'The Cognitive and Identity Development of Twins at Sixteen Years of Age: A Follow-up of Thirty-two Twin Pairs', in Christina Tinglof, *Parenting School Age Twins and Multiples*. New York: McGraw Hill Professional, 2007, 221.

Baumrind, Diana. 'Child Care Practices Anteceding Three Patterns of Preschool Behaviour'. *Genetic Psychology Monographs*, Vol. 75, No. 1, 1967, 43–88.

Baumrind, Diana. 'Effects of Authoritative Parental Control on Child Behavior'. *Child Development*, Vol. 37, No. 4, December 1966, 887–907.

Blair, Linda. 'The Secret Life of Brothers and Sisters: Five Lessons for Parents Who Want Their Children to Get On'. *Telegraph*, 12 July 2016.

Chamrad, D.L., Robinson, N.M. and Janos, P.M. 'Consequences of Having a Gifted Sibling: Myths and Realities'. *Gifted Child Quarterly*, Vol. 39 (3), 1995, 135–45.

Cicirelli, Victor G. 'Sibling Influence Throughout the Lifespan', in Michael E. Lamb and Brian Sutton-Smith, *Sibling Relationships: Their Nature and Significance Across the Lifespan*, Chapter 11, 267–84. New York: Psychology Press, 2009, 267–284.

Conger, Katherine, Stocker, Clare and McGuire, Shirley. 'Sibling Socialization: The Effects of Stressful Life Events and Experiences'. *New Directions in Child and Adolescent Development*, Vol. 2009, Issue 126, 45–59.

Herrick, Paige. 'Turning Points of Closeness in the Sibling Relationship'. Thesis submission, Department of Communication Studies, Baylor University, 15 April 2008. Davies, Betty. 'Long-Term Outcomes of Adolescent Sibling Bereavement'. *Journal of Adolescent Research*, Vol. 6, 1991, 83–96.

Fletcher, Jason, Mailick, Marsha, Song Jieun, and Wolfe, Barbara. 'A Sibling Death in the Family: Common and Consequential', *Demography*, 2013.

Gattis, Krista, Berns, Sara, Simpson, Lorelei E., and Christiansen, Andrew. 'Birds of a Feather or Strange Birds? Ties Among Personality Dimensions, Similarity, and Marital Quality', *Journal of Family Psychology*, Vol. 18 (4), 2004, 564–74.

Hinde, Robert A. 'On Describing Relationships', *Journal of Child Psychology and Psychiatry*, Vol. 17, No. 1, January 1976, 1–19.

Kempton, Tracy, Armistead, Lisa, Wierson, Michelle, and Forehand, Rex. 'Presence of a Sibling as a Potential Buffer Following Parental Divorce: An Examination of Young Adolescents', *Journal of Clinical Child Psychology*, Vol. 20 (4), 1991, 434–8.

Kichuk, S.L. and Weisner, W.H. 'The Big Five Personality Factors and Team Performance: Implications for Selecting Successful Product Design Teams', *Journal of Engineering and Technology*, Vol. 14 (3–4), 1997, 195–221.

Leduc, Rachelle. 'The Effects of Parental Separation and Divorce on Closeness in the Adult Sibling Relationship', undergraduate thesis, University of Portland, 2012.

Melby Gordon, Lynn. 'Twins and Kindergarten Separation: Divergent Beliefs of Principals, Teachers, Parents and Twins', *Education Policy*, Vol. 29 (4), 2014, 583–616.

Milevsky, Avidan. 'Perceived Parental Marital Satisfaction and Divorce', *Journal of Divorce and Remarriage*, Vol. 41 (1–2), 2004, 115–28.

Mischel, W. and Mischel, H.N. 'Development of Children's Knowledge of Self-Control Strategies', *Child Development*, Vol. 54, 1983, 603–19.

Nicoletti, Cheti and Rabe, Birgitta. 'Sibling Spillover Effects in School Achievement', Working Paper for the Institute of Social and Economic Research, October 2014.

Pison, G. and D'Addato, A.V. 'Frequency of Twin Births in Developed Countries', *Twin Research and Human Genetics*, Vol. 9 (2), April 2006.

Pison, G., Monden, C. and Smits, J. 'Twinning Rates in Developed Countries: Trends and Explanations', *Population and Development*, December 2015.

Renzulli, J.S. 'What Makes Giftedness? Re-examining a Definition', *Phi Beta Kappan*, Vol. 60 (3), 1978, 180–4.

Rosenthal, R. and Jacobson, L. 'Teachers' Expectancies: Determinants of Pupils' IQ Gains', *Psychological Reports*, Vol. 19 (1), 1966, 115–18.

Ross, Helgola G. and Milgram, Joel I. 'Important Variables in Adult Sibling Relationships: A Qualitative Study' in Michael E. Lamb and Brian Sutton-Smith (eds), *Sibling Relationships: Their Nature and Significance Across the Lifespan*, Chapter 9, pp. 225–49. New York: Psychology Press, 2009.

Simons, Ronald L., Beaman, Jay, Conger, Rand D. and Chao, Wei. 'Childhood Experience, Conceptions of Parenting, and Attitudes of Spouse as Determinants of Parental Behavior', *Journal of Marriage and Family*, Vol. 55, No. 1, February 1993, 91–106.

Simons, Ronald L., Whitbeck, Les, Conger, Rand D. and Wu, Chyi-in. 'Intergenerational Transmission of Harsh Parenting', *Developmental Psychology*, Vol. 27, No. 1, January 1991, 159–71.

Internet articles

Boyse, Kyla, University of Michigan Health System, October 2011: 'Your Child: Sibling Rivalry', www.med.umich.edu/yourchild/topics/sibriv. htm. Contains definitions, parental tips, and books on the subject for both parents and children.

Child Development Institute, 'Handling Sibling Rivalry', https://childdevelopmentinfo.com/ages-stages/school-age-children-development-parenting-tips/sibling_rivalry/#.WOOB8aJFfx8. Explanations and parenting tips.

North Carolina Cooperative Extension (Vickie Jones, Parenting Expert). 'Sibling Rivalry Can Help Teach Lessons'. www.ces.ncsu.edu, 7 February 2008.

Pamphlets

Sanders, Deidre, with Blair, Linda, Hayman, Suzie and Spurr, Pam. 'An Agony Aunt's Guide for Parting Parents and Their Children'. London: Department for Children, Schools and Families, 2008.

Anti-bullying charities

Bullying UK: www.bullying.co.uk
Childnet International: www.childnet.com
Contact a Family: www.cafamily.org.uk
The Diana Award: https://diana-award.org.uk
Family Lives: www.familylives.org.uk
Kidscape: www.kidscape.org.uk
NSPCC: www.nspcc.org.uk